Thanks for Talking Dirty with the Queen of Clean®

ALSO BY LINDA COBB

PRAISE FOR THE QUEEN OF CLEAN®

"Thanks for all your tips to clean up at home, while I try to clean up at the plate!"

—Luis Gonzalez,
Left fielder, Arizona Diamondbacks

"Linda Cobb, the self-styled Queen of Clean®, sweeps into the big time with spotless timing for a book on dirt. . . . *Talking Dirty with the Queen of Clean®* . . . has certainly cleaned up."

—*People* magazine

"There's no stain Linda Cobb can't tame."

—*New York Post*

"We thought we'd heard all the dirty talk for the Queen until a bagpipe-playing listener needed to clean the silver balls on his bagpipe thingy. With her encyclopedic knowledge, the Queen was able to get 'em all cleaned up. Linda is more than amazing . . . she's 'clean-a-rrific'!"

—*Beth and Bill in the Morning,*
KESZ-FM 99.9, Phoenix

"The Queen of Clean® has dug deep into her cleaning pail to find those elusive cleaning solutions. With this new book I never again will have to worry about a stain on my reputation."

—Tara Hitchcock, *Good Morning Arizona,*
KTVK-TV3, Phoenix

"In high school I was the scrub on the football team. It wasn't a compliment. The Queen of Clean®, however, has made me proud because with this new book, I can scrub anything clean!"

—Dan Davis, *Good Morning Arizona,*
KTVK-TV3, Phoenix

"There isn't any stain or cleaning problem for which Cobb doesn't have a solution."

—*Arizona Republic*

TALKING DIRTY

WITH THE QUEEN OF CLEAN®

NEW AND IMPROVED EDITION

LINDA COBB

POCKET BOOKS

New York   London   Toronto   Sydney

POCKET BOOKS, a division of Simon & Schuster, Inc.
1230 Avenue of the Americas, New York, NY 10020

Copyright © 1998, 2004 by Linda Cobb

Published by arrangement with The Win Holden Company

All rights reserved, including the right to reproduce
this book or portions thereof in any form whatsoever.
For information address The Win Holden Company,
6838 South 38th Place, Phoenix, AZ 85040

ISBN: 0-7434-9040-1

First Pocket Books trade paperback edition of this revised edition
April 2004

10 9 8 7 6

POCKET and colophon are registered trademarks of
Simon & Schuster, Inc.

Manufactured in the United States of America

Designed by Jaime Putorti

For information regarding special discounts for bulk purchases,
please contact Simon & Schuster Special Sales at 1-800-456-6798
or business@simonandschuster.com

Queen of Clean® is the registered trademark of Linda Cobb and is the
property of Queen and King Enterprises, Inc.

In memory of James Anthony Ranaldo, an amazing writer/producer and even better friend. All of us who were lucky enough to know you and work with you miss you, Jimmy.

THANK YOU

Over the years I have been fortunate to meet many people through my books and TV appearances. Many of you have been devoted to me and my natural cleaning tips for years. I have enjoyed meeting all of you and I thank each of you who took the time to tell me how one of my tips "saved your life" or helped you out of a sticky situation.

My heartfelt appreciation to all of my family and friends. Because of you, each day and in every way, it IS good to be Queen.

CONTENTS

INTRODUCTION

I t's been a long and heady ride. I can't quite believe it myself, but it's been years since I began talking dirty with you all. What started out as just one little appearance on a local television show has grown from a seed to a flower to a whole darn bouquet of opportunities. And speaking of opportunities, I'd like to take *this* one to thank all of you for sticking by me through thick and thin . . . dirty and clean!

My first book, *Talking Dirty with the Queen of Clean®*, hit the shelves in 1998. My purpose in bringing out that book was to give my fans a place to find all of my favorite cleaning tips and concoctions—the Queen's bible of cleaning, if you will. Of course I never regarded it as my "first book" at the time, because I never considered there would be another. But there was. And another. And another. And another. What fun talking dirty is! So here I am, six years and six books later, still cleaning up and still having fun doing it. Where does that leave us? Right back at the beginning, in fact!

Many things have changed since that first book. I've lost thirty pounds and two publicists. I've gone through 392 pairs of rubber gloves and 46 aprons. (And despite my best efforts, my editor still isn't married!) The Queen Mother has turned ninety and is still giving me advice. Sadly, Zack the Palace Pussy Cat is no longer with us, but Princess Zoe Elizabeth has taken up where Zack left off and has proved to be a great little research assistant in her own right.

In some ways it seems like the more things change, the more they stay the same; yet it also seems like the more things change . . . well, the more things change. Many cleaning products have come and gone, for example. Some old products still work, of course, but in other cases new products work even better. And, yes, there are new problems, too! Through contact with so many of my readers, I've encountered more problems and more stains, so I've come up with some new solutions and concoctions of my own. I mean, even a down-home Queen has to come into the twenty-first century . . . right?

So here it is: my new and improved version of my original housekeeping bible, *Talking Dirty with the Queen of Clean*®. For those of you who thought that Faster, Cheaper, and Easier was the name of a New York law firm, read on. This updated version of my tips, tricks, and treatments is still fun to leaf through. It's still easy to read. And it's still loaded with good advice. Once again I'm going to bring you the truth on what works and what doesn't. I'm going to help you determine what products should fly off the shelves and which should stay on, and I'm going to help you stretch your dollars, while keeping your sense. Basically, I've designed this book to help you find fun, fast, and frugal ways to keep a clean house. Because when it comes right down to it, we've *all* got better things to do than to clean house.

ARE YOU A DOMESTIC DIVA?

1. I should remove the zippered covers on my upholstered cushions
   a. before my mother-in-law, who still has the plastic on her furniture, comes to visit
   b. so I can put them in the washer
   c. never—they might shrink and then I'll be looking at foam instead of just a few spots

2. To make sure I can see my face in my chrome fixtures as well as my mirror, I
   a. spend at least an hour wiping them, making sure no spots are left
   b. use silver polish because they look silvery, right?
   c. give them a once-over with a dryer sheet

3. When my kitchen drain clogs up I
   a. call my plumber, that's why they have plumbers in the first place
   b. put on rubber gloves, a mask, and safety glasses and get out the most caustic substance I can find
   c. just open the cabinet, grab the salt and baking soda, and pour a cup of each down the drain, then add a kettle of boiling water

4. I smoke in my car and
   a. I cover up the smell with those pine-tree air fresheners
   b. I've just resigned myself to driving a portable ashtray
   c. I prevent the smell by putting baking soda in the ashtray and dryer sheets under the seats

5. I just painted my living room and
   a. now I'm scraping paint off light switches and doorknobs. Who knew I would be so messy?
   b. I laboriously wrapped layers and layers of tape all over every surface. It only took seventeen rolls
   c. I covered all the metal fixtures with petroleum jelly so any paint would just wipe off

6. I know that the easiest way to keep my copper pots shiny is to
   a. clean them regularly with special, expensive polish
   b. Shiny, who needs shiny? That greenish tinge looks nice . . . right?
   c. rub them with ketchup from the *free* ketchup packets I get from fast-food restaurants

7. I got so caught up in the horror flick I was watching (I think it was called *Attack of the Dirty Ovens*), I forgot about my microwave popcorn. Now the microwave reeks of burned popcorn, but not to worry
   a. microwaves don't weigh *that* much, I'll just move it to the back porch where it can air out for a few days
   b. I don't really mind that smell. Actually, it's so familiar that it says "home" to me
   c. I'll just microwave a bowl of water with some lemon slices to freshen it up

8. Speaking of dirty ovens, I think that mine is ready to attack.
   a. I had better go to the appliance store again. Time is money and I'd rather spend the cash than the time it will take me to clean that monster
   b. And I like it that way. Down and dirty in the kitchen is what I say
   c. I'll tame the beast with a simple paste of baking soda and ammonia

9. I'm prepared for the next time my husband "fixes" the car and makes an oily mess on the garage floor
   a. because I've already made up a bed for him on the couch. He knows what'll happen if he doesn't clean up after himself.
   b. because I've already listed that car in the want ads. No more car . . . no more mess
   c. because I know to take some of the Princess's Kitty Litter™ and sprinkle it on the spills. They'll be gone in no time

10. I've discovered a great way to keep myself healthy when everyone else in my office is passing around colds.
   a. I make sure to keep at least six feet between myself and my colleagues. I call it my safety zone
   b. I wear one of those surgical masks when I'm in public spaces. It may look strange, but it keeps me from feeling strange
   c. I wipe down my phone receiver with some Listerine®. My breath is fresh and my body is germ-free.

ANSWER KEY

Look at your answers and add up the number of times you chose each letter A, B, or C.

If you answered mostly A's: You're more than a domestic diva, you're an American Idol. It's surprising you had the time or energy to fill out this quiz! You're working too hard at keeping everything clean, though; brush up on some tips from the Queen so you can be more efficient . . . and more happy. Maybe it's time to come down off that pedestal.

If you answered mostly B's: You've reached the point of no return. Keeping up with all the cleaning has just become too much and you're resigned to taking the easiest route possible, which may mean doing nothing at all. Check out the Queen's tips for doing things quickly and easily . . . I promise, it's not as bad as you think.

If you answered mostly C's: You are the Queen of your domain! You've obviously taken the Queen's advice to heart and you're using it to keep your household under control . . . with as little fuss as possible. Keep it up—and recruit some friends!

ROYAL FLUSH

Over the years I have found that there is one room that generates question after question and that room is the bathroom.

Once, when I was eating in a wonderful little Chinese restaurant, the proprietor—an elderly Chinese gentleman—followed me into the ladies' room to see if I thought his bathrooms were clean. He was using the methods that I had recommended on television and was making his own cleanser from my recipe. Let me tell you, his bathrooms were spotless! It made me think that of all the rooms in your house, the bathroom is probably the room that most guests always see and have the most private time to observe. I have tried virtually every cleaning product on the market and developed many of my own "Queen's concoctions"—what follows are the best and easiest cleaning tips I can offer.

CLEANING PORCELAIN TUBS

To clean and polish a porcelain tub and remove stains, make a paste of powdered alum (available in drugstores) and water. Rub well, as if using cleanser. For stains, make a paste of powdered alum and lemon juice; apply and let dry, then moisten with more lemon juice and rub well. Rinse thoroughly.

Borax and water is also a great cleaner for porcelain. Make a paste and rub well, then rinse.

CLEANING FIBERGLAS™ SHOWERS AND TUBS

Heat white vinegar until it is hot, but not too hot to pour into a spray bottle and work with. Spray it on the shower and tub heavily. Wait 10–15 minutes and then moisten a scrubbing-type sponge with more of the vinegar and scrub down the shower, using additional heated vinegar as necessary. Rinse well and dry.

REMOVING HARD-WATER MARKS

Many plastic-type tubs have a dimpled, slip-proof bottom that defies cleaning. I have found that using a good gel cleaner or a mild cleanser, such as the homemade types listed on page 20, and a piece of fine drywall sandpaper (looks like window screen) works the best. Cut the sandpaper into a workable size, apply the cleaner, and rub. Use this only on dimples in plastic and Fiberglas™ tub and shower bottoms.

STUBBORN SPOT REMOVER FOR SHOWERS

For stubborn shower spots and scum buildup, use a dry, soap-filled steel-wool pad on a dry shower. Do not allow water to become involved in this process, as it will cause the steel-wool pad to scratch. Follow up with the vinegar process described on page 2.

KEEPING PLASTIC SHOWERS CLEAN

To make shower upkeep simple, apply a coat of car wax. Do not use this on the floor of the tub or shower. After showering, use a squeegee to wipe down the shower door and walls, and your shower will stay clean and you'll have fewer problems with mildew.

KEEPING TILE AND GROUT CLEAN

You can keep ahead of grout cleaning if you use a dry type-writer eraser on dry grout to remove mildew and stains as they appear. For bigger problems, make a paste of baking soda and chlorine bleach and apply to the grout. Let dry and then rinse. Do this in a well-ventilated area, using care near carpet or fabric. Even the fumes of chlorine bleach can remove color from towels left hanging in the tub area.

TILE AND GROUT CLEANER

Combine 2 parts baking soda, 1 part borax, and 1 part hot water, adding additional water as necessary to form a thick paste. Apply to the tile and grout, and scrub with a soft brush. Rinse well.

This is a handy spray-on grout cleaner for frequent use, good for removing soap scum and cleaning tile counters:

½ cup of baking soda

⅓ cup of ammonia

¼ cup of white vinegar

7 cups of water

Combine all the ingredients in a labeled spray bottle and shake well to mix. Do not use this in conjunction with chlorine bleach or where chlorine bleach has been used. Simply spray it on and then wipe with a damp sponge or cloth. No rinsing required.

REMOVING SOAP SCUM FROM GLASS SHOWER DOORS

Removing soap and scum buildup on glass shower doors is always tedious. Lemon oil or even plain old mineral oil will remove it quickly and easily, and will help to keep it from coming back. Apply the oil to a rough cloth, such as an old washcloth, and rub it across the dirty shower door surface. Next buff with a soft cloth or paper towels to provide a haze-free shine. The oil provides a protective coating that keeps the water beading and the soap scum from adhering. Never put oil or allow it to drip on the floor of the shower; this will prevent good traction in the shower and may cause someone to fall.

CLEANING SOAP SCUM AND MILDEW OFF PLASTIC SHOWER CURTAINS

Put the shower curtain in the washing machine with 1 cup of white vinegar, ¼ to ½ cup of your favorite liquid laundry detergent, and several old, light-colored towels. Fill the washer with warm water and run through complete wash and rinse cycle. Remove from the washer and hang on the shower rod immediately.

CLEANING MINERAL DEPOSITS FROM THE SHOWERHEAD

Fill a plastic sandwich bag with undiluted white vinegar. Tie this around the showerhead and leave overnight. In the morning, remove the bag, scrub the head with a brush, and it's ready to use.

Put ½ cup of baking soda down the bathroom drain and follow with the vinegar from the plastic bag—great drain opener! Wait 30 minutes, then flush with water.

CLEANING CHROME FAUCETS

Use white vinegar on a cloth or sponge to remove water spots and soap scum. Dry and buff with a soft cloth. Rubbing alcohol is also a great spot remover. Apply, then dry and buff.

To shine chrome or any metal fixture in a hurry, use a used dryer fabric-softener sheet on a dry fixture.

Apply some lemon juice to chrome fixtures and buff with a soft cloth to a brilliant shine.

REMOVING HAIR SPRAY RESIDUE

You can use this formula to remove hair spray residue from any hard surface—vanities, tile, floors, walls, etc. Mix a solution of ⅓ liquid fabric softener and ⅔ water in a spray bottle. Spray on the surface to be cleaned and wipe. Not only does it remove hair spray, it also acts as a dust repellent and shines vanities beautifully!

Mix 50 percent rubbing alcohol and 50 percent water in a spray bottle and use it to remove styling product residue.

REMOVING BATHTUB DECALS

Lay a sheet of aluminum foil over the decals and heat with a blow-dryer on high. Work up the edge of the decal with a dull straightedge (credit cards work great) and keep applying the heat as you pull. If the decal is stubborn, lay down the foil as necessary and heat well and peel again. To remove the residue, try petroleum jelly, denatured alcohol, or nail polish remover. Test these products in a small area first before applying.

PALACE PENNYSAVERS

HAIR TODAY Dilute your shampoo and conditioner with water to save, save, save. No need to watch all that money go down the drain!

CLEANING SHOWER DOOR TRACKS

Plug the drain holes in the door track with a little bit of paper towel made into a ball. Pour in undiluted white vinegar. Let this soak for 30 minutes, unplug the holes, rinse the track with a spray bottle of water, and run a rag down it. This will flush the accumulated buildup out of the track.

TOILET TIPS

If you have indoor plumbing, then you have to clean the toilet once in a while, whether you like it or not. Follow these tips and it will be a breeze:

Tang® Tune-up

To keep your toilet clean and your dog happy, put several tablespoons of Tang® Breakfast Drink in the toilet before you leave for work or at bedtime. Let it soak, use your toilet brush to swish around under the rim, and flush. The great thing about this is you don't have to worry if the kids get into the toilet bowl cleaner.

Removing Hard-Water Rings

Shut off the water at the toilet tank and flush. Spray undiluted white vinegar around the inside of the toilet, then sprinkle borax onto the vinegar. Let soak about 30 minutes and then scrub with a piece of fine drywall sandpaper (looks like window screen—available at hardware stores and home centers). If you have an old hard-water ring, you may need to repeat this several times.

Plop-Plop-Fizz-Fizz Cleaning

Drop a couple of denture-cleaning tablets into the toilet and let sit overnight. Brush under the rim with your bowl brush and flush.

To clean stubborn stains from a toilet bowl, first shut off the water at the tank and flush the toilet to remove as much water as possible. Combine in a bucket:

1 tablespoon ammonia

1 cup of 3 percent hydrogen peroxide (drugstore variety)

1½ quarts water

Pour the solution in the toilet bowl and use a brush to apply it to the sides of the bowl. Let stand at least 30 minutes, then scrub the inside of the bowl with a scrub brush. Allow to remain in the toilet for up to several hours, reapplying the solution to the sides of the bowl frequently as needed. Do not use this with chlorine bleach or products that contain chlorine bleach. This solution cleans and disinfects.

A woman called in to a radio show I was on to find out how to remove a varnish-like substance from her bathroom walls, vanity, shelves, mirror, virtually everywhere in the bathroom. I immediately asked what type of varnish it was, had a can of it spilled, and how old was it. She said she didn't know. They had just moved into this house and the whole bathroom looked like it had been misted with varnish. As my mind worked to find a cure, I suddenly said to her, did a teenage girl use the bathroom? She said yes. Being a woman who as a teenager used every styling product known to man and a can of Aqua Net® hair spray a day, I immediately suggested that her problem was a buildup of styling-product residue. I suggested that she combine 1 part liquid fabric softener with 2 parts water in a spray bottle. Spray any hard surface, let sit a few minutes, and then wipe or use a nylon scrubbing sponge to remove the sticky residue. Then rinse. Before the program ended she called back to say that the "varnish" was gone.

2

KITCHEN DUTY

don't think there is a room in the house that gets messy
faster than the kitchen. So let's clean up!

APPLIANCE MAGIC

Many of us have white appliances in the kitchen. To keep
them from yellowing, try this formula when you clean the
exterior.

Combine:

8 cups water

½ cup chlorine bleach

½ cup baking soda

2 tablespoons borax

Wash white appliances thoroughly (using care around carpet or fabric), rinse well, and dry.

- Rubbing alcohol makes a great cleaner for the exterior of all types of appliances. Use care around flames.
- Club soda is a wonderful polish for the exterior of appliances. It doesn't have to be fresh and have fizz; even if it has lost its carbonation it works great.
- Don't grab your everyday dishcloth to wipe down appliances; it will transfer grease and smear the finish.

CUTTING BOARDS

Remove odors from breadboards by wetting and then rubbing with a little dry mustard. Let sit for a few minutes and then rinse. To disinfect breadboards, especially wood, keep a spray bottle with 1 quart water and 3 teaspoons of liquid chlorine bleach. Spray on, let sit at least 5 minutes, and then rinse with hot water.

For a great cleaner and stain remover, apply lemon juice to the board, let sit 15 minutes, then rinse and dry well. This works particularly well on wood cutting boards.

BROILER PAN

For quick, easy, neat cleaning, put the broiler pan in a plastic garbage bag and lay some paper towels on it. Spray with ammonia, close bag, and leave overnight. In the morning, open bag (away from face, remember the fumes), wipe with the towels that are in the bag, remove, wash broiler pan, and throw out the rest of the mess.

BURNED-ON CASSEROLES

Fill the casserole or pan with hot water and throw in several used dryer fabric-softener sheets. Let soak (even overnight), rinse, and wash.

A handful of baking soda and some hot water will also work well.

AUTOMATIC COFFEEMAKERS

Depending on how often you use your coffeepot and how hard your water is, you may want to do this once a month to once every 3 months.

Fill the water reservoir with undiluted white vinegar. Place a filter in the coffee basket and turn the pot on. Allow about half of the vinegar to run through and then shut off the pot. Let it sit for about 30 minutes, then turn the coffeemaker on and allow the balance of the vinegar to run through. Clean the pot out well, fill the reservoir with fresh, cold water, and allow it to run through. Run the fresh water through twice.

To Clean the Glass Pot

Use lemon and salt and rub with a sponge, or use baking soda and lemon juice or water and rub with a sponge. Rinse well.

To Clean the Basket and Other Parts

For white plastic units, soak any removable parts in hot water with dishwashing liquid and about ¼ cup of chlorine bleach. Soak about 30 minutes and rinse well. This helps remove the staining and oils. For dark-colored coffeemakers, use dishwashing liquid and about ¼ cup of white vinegar in the same manner as above.

CHROME BURNER RINGS AND GUARDS

Remove the burner rings from the stove. Lay a single sheet of paper toweling on each pan and moisten with ammonia. Place them in a plastic bag and close the bag. Leave for several hours or overnight. Open bag (pointed away from face, please) and remove the parts. Wash, rinse, and dry.

DISHWASHERS

To remove that milky film from glassware and clean the inside of your dishwasher, follow this procedure.

Fill the dishwasher with your glassware (no metal, please). Use no dishwasher detergent. Put a bowl in the bottom of the dishwasher and pour in 1 cup of household bleach. Run through the wash cycle, but do not dry. Fill the bowl again with 1 cup

Want an easy way to freshen up that dishcloth? Just run it through the dishwasher the next time you do a load. Works for sponges, too!

white vinegar and let the dishwasher go through the entire cycle. Now you have the film removed from your dishes and the dishwasher clean in one easy step.

Remember, if you allow the film to build up for too long, it will permanently etch the glass.

Dishwasher Odor

Sprinkle borax in the bottom of the dishwasher and leave it overnight. Using a damp sponge, wipe down the inside of the dishwasher, door, and gaskets with the borax. No need to rinse, just do the next load of dishes.

Dishwasher Rust

To remove rust from the inside of the dishwasher, fill both detergent cups with Tang® Breakfast Drink and run through the normal cycle. If rust is bad, several treatments may be required. When doing this, don't put dishes or detergent in the dishwasher.

Dishwasher Spot Stopper

To keep your dishes spot-free, use this formula. Combine the following ingredients in a container with a lid:

    1 cup borax
    ½ cup baking soda

To use: Add 1 teaspoon of the mixture to the dishwasher along with your regular dishwasher detergent.

THE PAIN OF DRAINS

This is the best nontoxic drain opener you will ever use. Pour 1 cup of salt (table salt, rock salt—any kind) and 1 cup of baking soda down the drain. Follow with a kettle of boiling water. If the problem is congealed grease, it will be gone immediately. For the very best results, don't use the drain for several hours. If you need a stronger product, use 2 tablespoons of washing soda (available where laundry products are sold) dissolved in 1 quart of hot water, and pour it slowly down the drain. Flush with hot water after 10 minutes.

CLEANING THE DISPOSAL

Keep your garbage disposal clean and free-flowing by filling the sink with 3 inches of warm water and mixing in 1 cup of baking soda. Drain it with the disposal running.

USING THE PLUNGER THE EASY WAY

Yes, there really is a special way to use a plunger to make it work more effectively. Close the overflow to the sink (usually in the front of the sink) by plugging it with an old rag. If you don't do this, the water will go down one hole and come back up the overflow. Fill the sink with 4–5 inches of water. Put the cup of the plunger over the drain and press down hard. Then pull the handle up, push down again, and repeat 10–12 times. Adding a little petroleum jelly around the rim of the plunger gives even better suction.

PALACE PENNYSAVERS

ONCE-A-MONTH DRAIN CLEANER Once a month, pour a handful of baking soda into the drain and add ½ cup of white vinegar. A small volcano will erupt. Cover the drain for several minutes, then flush with cold water after 30 minutes.

MICROWAVE MAGIC

You have probably seen the microwave cleaning products that are on the market. You place a pouch in the microwave, microwave it for a minute or so, leave the door closed for a while, then remove the pouch, take out the wipe inside it, and wipe out the microwave. These cost approximately 60 cents per pouch. Do they work? Yes, with the power of steam cleaning. Do you need or want to spend that kind of money? Of course not! Here are some much easier and less expensive ways to achieve the same results.

To clean your microwave quickly and simply, wet a dishcloth, leaving it fairly wet, and place it in the center of your microwave. Turn on high and allow the cloth to sort of cook for about 45–60 seconds. The steam that this creates will help loosen any hardened spills, and you can then use the heated cloth to wipe the inside clean. A note of caution: Don't try to use the cloth immediately; it will be very hot. This is a great way to disinfect your dishcloth, too.

DEODORIZING THE MICROWAVE

To give your microwave a clean, fresh smell, place a bowl of water in it and add 3 or 4 slices of fresh lemon or 2 tablespoons of lemon juice. Cook on high for 30–60 seconds.

For the very worst odors, such as burned popcorn, place vanilla extract in a bowl and microwave for at least 30 seconds. Leave the door closed for 12 hours, remove the vanilla, and wipe down the inside of the microwave.

If all else fails, put some ODORZOUT™ in a bowl and sit it in the microwave, leaving the door cracked for air circulation. Leave inside 24–48 hours.

THE SMOKING OVEN

When something runs over in the oven and starts smoking and smelling, grab the salt. Sprinkle on a heavy layer of salt and continue cooking. The smoke and odor will stop immediately. When done cooking, close the oven and wait overnight. The next day you will be able to lift out the spill with a pancake turner!

AN OUNCE OF PREVENTION

BY THE BOOK I'm as impatient as the next Queen, but let me tell you, taking a few minutes to read the instructions that come with new products and appliances will prevent hours of aggravation.

CLEANING THE OVEN

Preheat oven to 200 degrees and leave on for 15 minutes. Shut off and leave door closed. Fill a shallow glass dish with ammonia and place on the top shelf. On the lower shelf place a pan filled with 2 cups of boiling water. Close the oven door and leave the pans inside 2 hours or overnight. Remove ammonia and water; make a paste of ammonia, ½ cup baking soda, and 1 cup white vinegar. Spread paste over surfaces and leave on for about 15 minutes. Scrub with a sponge and steel-wool pad (if necessary), then rinse. This even works on heavily soiled ovens.

MAKING YOUR OWN CLEANSER

For a great nonabrasive scouring powder for disinfecting, combine:

> 4 parts baking soda
> 1 part borax
> Store in a shaker container.

For a nontoxic grease-cutting scouring powder, combine:

> 4 parts baking soda
> 1 part washing soda
> Store in a shaker container.

CLEANING AND PROTECTING COOKTOPS

I receive so many questions about cleaning cooktops that I decided to devote a section just to that. Actually, glass and smooth-top ceramic surfaces are fairly easy to clean if you follow a few rules when dealing with them.

Clean the surface only when it is cool, with either dishwashing liquid, a paste of baking soda and water (3 parts baking soda to 2 parts water), or a specially formulated cooktop cleaner. Apply this with a paper towel or soft cloth.

Rinse thoroughly and towel dry. Do not use a soiled dishcloth or sponge to wipe the top; it may leave a film, which can cause discoloration the next time it is heated. If this discoloration occurs, remove it with a specially formulated cooktop cleaner.

I keep an ACT Natural® Microfiber Cloth for just cleaning my stovetop. Wet the cloth, wring out well, wipe to remove soiling, and buff with a paper towel. This leaves no product haze on the stove surface.

Burned-on soil can be removed with a razor-blade scraper. Avoid abrasive cleaners and pads.

If your cooktop is in really bad shape, you will have to take more drastic action before you can have cleaning ease.

You can try a product called Bon Ami®, which comes in a can, much like cleanser. This product can safely be used on mirrors, windows, windshields, etc. It has a mild pumice action. Use it carefully with a soft, wet rag to remove heavy soiling. You can also use a mild ammonia solution along with a scrubbing-type sponge. Another product that will help remove stains and burned-on food is nongel toothpaste, applied with a soft cloth.

Follow up these cleaning procedures by washing with dishwashing liquid and water and rinsing well. Rinsing with club soda will put a nice shine on the top surface.

REFRIGERATOR ODORS AND SPILLS

When you wipe out the refrigerator, always use a cloth or sponge moistened with white vinegar. It leaves a clean, fresh scent and helps prevent mildew.

A dab of vanilla, lemon, or orange extract on a small pad of cotton will keep the refrigerator fresh-smelling without a perfume odor.

Many common refrigerator odors may be removed by placing a small tub filled with charcoal in the middle rack in the refrigerator. I use the charcoal made for fish tanks.

If you are shutting off a refrigerator, be sure to prop the door open a crack with a stick for air circulation and put a container of fresh coffee grounds inside to ward off unpleasant odors. For strong-odor removal, a container or nylon stocking with coffee grounds in it works wonders. Be sure to childproof the refrigerator

QUICK TIP

To remove stains from nonstick cookware, boil 2 tablespoons of baking soda, ½ cup of white vinegar, and 1 cup of water for 10–15 minutes. Reseason the pan with salad oil.

by putting a heavy tie around it to hold the door tightly against the stick to keep a child from climbing in and being locked inside.

For cleaning ease, wipe the inside of the refrigerator, including shelves, with a cloth dipped in glycerin, available in the hand cream section at the drugstore. This light coating will keep spills from sticking. Even milk or sticky substances will wipe right out.

Also apply a light coating of petroleum jelly to the door gasket to keep it from drying out and cracking.

AN OUNCE OF PREVENTION

ICE AGE Ice trays won't stick to the freezer if you put down a layer of waxed paper.

YIELD

FREEZERS

Try using the glycerin in freezers, too. That way spills, even though frozen, wipe right out.

Wash out the freezer with a solution of 1 gallon warm water and ¼ cup borax to clean and deodorize. Rinse and dry.

CLEANING STAINLESS STEEL CUTLERY

This is such an easy way to clean your stainless steel cutlery (forks, knives, spoons). Mix the following ingredients in the kitchen sink or any nonaluminum container:

¼ cup chlorine bleach

¼ cup Calgon Water Softener®

1 gallon very hot water

Immerse stainless steel cutlery in the solution for 30 minutes and wash as usual. This is not for use on real silver.

To remove stubborn spots from stainless steel, use a little nongel toothpaste or some silver polish in a separate container with a little ammonia added to it. Apply this with a soft cloth; wash, rinse, and dry.

CLEANING SILVER CUTLERY

Wash silver cutlery as soon as possible after using. This prevents tarnish-causing stains. To clean a lot of silver cutlery quickly:

Put strips of aluminum foil in a large bowl. Place the silver cutlery on top. Cover the cutlery with boiling water and add 3 tablespoons of baking soda.

Soak for 10 minutes, rinse, and dry. Use care on hollow or glued pieces. Also works on silver jewelry.

You can also make your own silver-cleaning cloths. Saturate cotton squares in a solution of:

2 parts ammonia

1 part silver polish

10 parts cold water

Let cloths drip dry and use as silver polish cloths.

AN OUNCE OF PREVENTION

A WORD OF WARNING Never wash stainless steel and silver cutlery together. It will cause the silver to pit.

STAINLESS STEEL SINKS

So much of my mail asks about cleaning and keeping up the appearance of stainless steel sinks. One such writer suggested using the sink as an ugly planter and using nothing but paper plates and plastic silverware! Take heart—here are ways to keep them clean and actually enjoy them.

Regular Cleaning

Clean with a paste of baking soda and water and rinse well. Drying the sink helps to prevent water marks and rust.

Polishing

Polish with flour. Put a tablespoon of flour in a dry sink and rub with a soft cloth. Then rinse and dry. Another polish method is club soda. Put the stopper in the sink, pour in some club soda, and rub with a soft cloth. Again, dry to prevent water spots.

Removing Rust and Water Spots

Use white vinegar on a soft cloth or sponge. It will not only erase the spots, but will also brighten the sink. Rubbing alcohol or lighter fluid will also remove rust marks. Remember the flammability of lighter fluid and use with care.

Removing Stains

Prepare a paste of 3 parts of cream of tartar to 1 part hydrogen peroxide and apply it to the stains. Allow it to dry and then wipe with a wet cloth or sponge.

To Shine

Coat the sink with a few drops of lemon, almond, or baby oil. Wipe it off with paper towels. If it doesn't seem shiny enough, repeat the procedure.

Erasing Hairline Scratches

Using very fine steel wool, gently give the entire sink the once-over to obliterate hairline scratches. Then wash and buff with a soft cloth.

METAL CLEANERS

Here are some fast, easy, homemade metal cleaners. Always test in an inconspicuous spot before using.

Aluminum

Combine:
- ½ cup baking soda
- ½ cup cream of tartar
- ½ cup white vinegar
- ¼ cup soap flakes

First combine the baking soda and cream of tartar, then add the white vinegar (foaming is normal) and mix well. Add the soap flakes and mix well again. Store in a glass jar or plastic container with a sturdy lid and label clearly. To use: Dip a piece of 0000 (fine) steel wool into the solution and apply to aluminum in a circular motion. Rinse well.

Brass

Use a mixture of lemon juice and salt. Wipe on until clean, then rinse and dry. Not for use on brass-plated pieces.

Copper

Use ketchup or Worcestershire sauce. Wipe on, rub until clean, rinse, and buff.

Gold

On small pieces use nongel toothpaste and a soft brush, such as a toothbrush. Rinse well. Any household ammoniated cleaner mixed 50/50 with water also works well.

Chrome

Rub with aluminum foil wrapped around your finger or hand, or wipe with a dry, used dryer fabric-softener sheet.

THE QUEEN'S BEST KITCHEN QUICK TIPS

USING YOUR MARBLES
When using your double boiler, drop several marbles in with the water. If it should start to boil dry, the marbles will rattle, alerting you to the problem before the pan is ruined.

- To remove food odors from plastic containers, fill with warm water and add a little dry mustard—¼ teaspoon is plenty for an average-size container. Let soak for an hour or so and then wash.

- To remove stains from plastic, put the open container in the sun. For stubborn spots, brush with a little lemon juice first.

- To chase away the odor of burned foods, boil some lemon slices or 1 tablespoon of bottled lemon juice in a saucepan for a few minutes.

- To chase away the odor of fried foods, even fish, place a small bowl of white vinegar next to the stove as you are frying.

- Adding a tablespoon of vinegar to water before poaching those eggs will prevent the whites from spreading.

- Clean porcelain pieces and the sink by filling the sink with warm water and adding several denture-cleaning tablets.
- To remove stains from a countertop, massage a paste of cream of tartar and lemon juice into the stain, let it soak, then rinse.
- Clean and sanitize your sponge and dishcloth by wedging them into the dishwasher and washing them along with a load of dishes. You can also wet the sponge or dishcloth and put it in the microwave for 30 seconds.
- To remove grease from wooden cupboards, apply a thin coat of car wax, let it dry, and buff.
- Remove plastic stuck to toasters with a little nail polish remover. Be sure toaster is unplugged.
- Store your steel-wool pad in the freezer each time you finish with it and it will never rust. Just tuck it into a sandwich bag.
- To clean a scorched pan, fill with warm water and add several tablespoons of baking soda. Boil until the scorched parts loosen and float to the surface.
- Remove rust from baking pans by rubbing with cleanser and a cut raw potato.
- Spray a grater with nonstick cooking spray before using and cleanup will be a breeze.
- Crack an egg at an angle and you're less likely to break the yolk.
- Clean the outside of a cast-iron pan with oven

cleaner. Clean the inside by boiling a solution of water and a couple of tablespoons of white vinegar in it. Reseason with cooking oil and store with a piece of waxed paper in it after each use. Never wash the inside of the pan with soap.

Does that recipe call for honey? Spray your measuring spoon with nonstick cooking spray before using and cleanup will be a snap!

- To clean the inside of a thermos, fill with warm water and add 1 teaspoon of chlorine bleach. Let soak 30–60 minutes and rinse well.
- Preserve wooden salad bowls by wiping with a paper towel soaked in cooking oil. This prevents drying and cracking. Do not immerse in water for more than just a few seconds to clean. Always dry thoroughly.
- Remove rust from a knife or other kitchen utensil by sticking it in an onion for about an hour. Move the piece back and forth to help the onion juice do its work.
- Always put glass dishes into hot water sideways and they will never break from the expansion and contraction.

If you or someone you love has asthma or allergies, you know the horror of opening cleaning products and having an attack. Try using the ACT Natural® Microfiber Cloths instead of cleaning chemicals. These cloths use nothing but water to clean and actually capture and contain 99.5 percent of dirt and bacteria so that you can wash them down the drain. The cloths can be used in the kitchen and bathroom for cleaning showers, tubs, sinks, fixtures, counters—any hard surface. Use them in your car, to spot-clean clothes you are wearing—they have a multitude of uses. The glass and crystal cloth allows you to polish windows, mirrors, glass, and crystal to a brilliant, streak-free shine. The mop has a dry head and a wet head that are attached with ease to the mop-holder with hook-and-eye tape. Again you are using no chemicals or soaps and leaving no residue on surfaces or chemicals in the air you breathe. When you are done with the cloths or mop head, toss them in the washing machine for clean, fresh cloths and mop each time you use them. They come with a two-year warranty. Check them out at www.actnatural.net.

3

CLEANING PRODUCTS YOU SHOULD NEVER BE WITHOUT

There are five cleaning products you should never be without, and most of them are things you already have in your home. You can purchase generous-size containers of all of them for a total of $10 and they will last for months. They can be used alone, together, or in conjunction with other common household products such as salt or dishwashing liquid to help you handle most of the cleaning problems in your home. They are especially good for people with allergies and those of us who want to cut back on the chemicals in our homes.

Now we'll take them in order and talk about their many uses.

Here's Your Shopping List
White Vinegar
Baking Soda
Lemon Juice
Club Soda
20 Mule Team® Borax

WHITE VINEGAR

Use white vinegar to remove heavy soap scum and mineral deposits from showers, tubs, and sinks. Warm the vinegar and put in a spray bottle. Spray on showers, tubs, and sinks and let soak for 10–15 minutes. Then use a nylon scrubbing sponge to remove scum. Respray if necessary. To remove mineral deposits from around drains, close drain and pour in enough white vinegar to cover the drain area. Let soak overnight, scrub with a nylon scrubbing sponge, drain vinegar, and rinse.

To remove scum and mineral buildup from showerheads and keep them free-flowing, put undiluted white vinegar in a plastic bag. Tie around the showerhead overnight. Scrub head and poke any loosened mineral deposits with a toothpick, rinse, and enjoy your next shower.

To remove soap scum and mildew from plastic shower curtains and liners, fill the washing machine with warm water, 1 cup of white vinegar, and your regular laundry detergent. Add the curtains, along with several old, light-colored towels. Run through complete cycle and rehang curtains immediately.

Add 2–3 tablespoons white vinegar to hot water along with your regular dishwashing liquid to cut grease on dishes and crystal.

Add ¼ cup of white vinegar to the washing machine during the final rinse to soften clothes and remove lint from dark clothes.

Apply, undiluted, to the skin with a cotton ball to deter bugs—they hate the way you taste, but the odor disappears immediately from your skin.

Neutralize pet urine odor with diluted white vinegar (25 percent vinegar to 75 percent water) sprayed on carpets. Always test in an inconspicuous spot before treating a large area.

Clean stainless steel sinks with a paste of baking soda and vinegar. Don't let the foaming scare you—it works great!

Make a window cleaner in a spray bottle with 1/4 cup white vinegar added to 1 quart of water.

Make air freshener in a spray bottle with 1 teaspoon of baking soda, 1 tablespoon of white vinegar, and 2 cups of water. After the foaming stops, put on lid. Shake before using.

Clean vinyl floors with ½ cup white vinegar to 1 gallon of warm water.

Keep drains free-flowing with ½ cup baking soda and

½ cup white vinegar poured down the drain monthly. After pouring in baking soda and vinegar, cover the drain for 15 minutes (it will foam). Then flush with cold water.

Clean mirrors with a solution of half vinegar and half water. Wet a sponge, soft cloth, or paper towel, wash, then buff dry. Never spray water onto a mirror. Moisture that gets into the edges and behind mirrors ruins the silvering on the mirror, resulting in dark spots.

Spray vinegar on the underarms of clothes and let soak 15–30 minutes to deodorize and minimize underarm stains.

Make an excellent toilet cleaner with 1 cup borax and 1 cup vinegar. Pour the vinegar over the stained area of the toilet, then sprinkle the borax over the vinegar. Soak for 2 hours and then brush and flush.

BAKING SODA

Baking soda is a great deodorizer, cleaner, and mild abrasive. Use as you would a soft-scrubbing product or cleanser in tubs and sinks.

Keep food disposals fresh and free-flowing by putting the stopper in the disposal and adding 3 inches of warm water and a handful of baking soda. Turn on the disposal and let water run out.

Remove perspiration stains and odor from clothing by

applying a paste of baking soda and water and letting it soak 30 minutes prior to laundering.

Mix 1 gallon of warm water and ¼ cup of baking soda. Soak freshly washed socks in this for 30 minutes. Spin out in the washer (do not rinse out the solution), dry, and you will have odor-eater socks.

Clean smudges on wallpaper with baking soda and water.

Remove crayon from hard surfaces with baking soda on a damp rag.

Use on any hard surface as a mild abrasive to remove stains.

Use as a bug killer for aphids. Use 1½ teaspoons of baking soda per pint of water and apply every 7 days.

To clean grout (any color), mix 3 cups of baking soda with 1 cup of warm water. Scrub grout with a brush and rinse.

Use baking soda on a damp cloth to polish silver.

To remove burned food in casseroles, fill dish with hot water and add 1 tablespoon of baking soda and allow to soak.

To clean up pet vomit, sprinkle on a heavy coating of baking soda. Let it absorb moisture and dry, then scoop or vacuum up. The baking soda will neutralize acids and help prevent stains. Follow with your favorite carpet spotter.

Remove heel marks from hard floors with a damp cloth and baking soda.

Clean screen stain and mineral deposits off windows by dipping a soft, wet cloth in baking soda and rubbing gently. Follow by washing windows as usual.

Remove streaks and greasy film from car windshields with a thin paste of baking soda and water. Rinse well.

Put in the bottom of cat litter boxes to help eliminate odor. Put in a thin layer of baking soda, then add the litter as usual. This works with clay or clumping varieties.

LEMON JUICE

Lemon juice is nature's bleach and disinfectant.

Apply to clothes, undiluted, to remove fruit-based stains. Let soak 30 minutes and then launder.

Remove rust from clothes by applying undiluted lemon juice and laying the garment in the sun. It disappears like magic.

Bleach spots off Formica® counters by using straight or mixing in a paste with baking soda.

Clean brass and copper with lemon juice and salt. Sprinkle salt on half a lemon and rub metal, then rinse thoroughly. If you don't have fresh lemons, you can also mix bottled lemon juice and salt.

Make a cleaner in a spray bottle with 2 cups of water, 2 tablespoons of lemon juice, ½ teaspoon of liquid dish soap, 1 tablespoon of baking soda, and 1 teaspoon of borax. Shake before using to clean any hard surface.

Apply lemon juice to chrome and buff to a shine.

As a bleach alternative, use ¼ cup of lemon juice and ¼ cup of white vinegar mixed in 1 gallon of warm water, and soak clothes for 15 minutes prior to washing.

Remove stains from hands with lemon juice.

Bleach wooden breadboards by applying lemon juice and letting them sit overnight. Wash and rinse in the morning.

PALACE PENNYSAVERS

Check the unit price before shelling out for that *large, economy size*. Often that thrifty size isn't so thrifty at all!

CLUB SODA

Club soda is the best emergency spotter there is. Keep club soda on hand to clean up spills on carpet and clothing. Remember to react as soon as possible to a spill. If you act fast, a spot shouldn't become a stain. Club soda will remove red wine, coffee, tea, pop (yes, even red pop!), Kool-Aid®, and any other spills you can think of. Lift any solids carefully off carpet or clothes and then pour on the club soda, blotting with an old rag until all the color from the spill is removed. Don't be afraid to really wet the carpet, it won't hurt it—carpet goes through countless dippings in water as it is made. Blot carpet easily by folding a rag and standing on it, turning the rag as it absorbs moisture and discoloration from the spill. The carbonation in the club soda brings the offending spill to the surface so that you can blot it up, and the salts in it will help prevent staining.

If you spill something on your clothes in a restaurant, ask for a little club soda or seltzer and use your napkin to blot the stain until it is removed. At home you can pour the club soda directly onto the spot, flushing it out.

I have found that club soda will work on many old stains, too. Always keep several bottles on hand.

20 MULE TEAM® BORAX

Now's your chance to harness the power of twenty mules for general cleaning and laundry. Borax is a natural additive that will boost the cleaning power of your regular laundry detergent and deodorize your laundry, too. But don't stop there. It is amazing for all kinds of cleaning. Look for 20 Mule Team® Borax in the laundry additive section at grocery and discount stores.

Borax and water is a great cleaner for porcelain bathroom fixtures. Make a paste, and rub well, then rinse.

Combine 2 parts baking soda, 1 part borax, and 1 part hot water to make a fantastic grout cleaner. Mix together and, using a brush, rub into the grout. Rinse well when you are done.

Remove hard-water rings from toilets by shutting the water off at the tank and flushing the toilet to remove as much water as possible. Spray the toilet bowl with heated white vinegar and then sprinkle on borax. Use a piece of fine drywall sandpaper to remove the ring. Turn the water back on and flush for a sparkling toilet bowl.

To clean white appliances, combine 8 cups of water, ½ cup of chlorine bleach, ½ cup of baking soda, and 2 table-spoons of borax. Wash white appliances thoroughly (using care around carpets and fabrics), rinse well, and dry.

To keep dishwashers odor free, use a damp sponge and some borax to wipe out the inside of the dishwasher, door, and gaskets. No need to rinse, just do the next load of dishes.

To make your own dishwasher spot stopper, combine the following ingredients in a container with a lid: 1 cup of borax and ½ cup of baking soda. To use: Add 1 teaspoon of the mixture to the dishwasher along with your regular dish-washer detergent.

Make your own nonabrasive scouring powder by com-bining 4 parts baking soda and 1 part borax. Store in a labeled shaker container.

To clean vinyl floors, mop with a mixture of 1 gallon of warm water and 1 tablespoon of borax. This will maintain the shine on floors, even those that are waxed.

To remove odor from training pants and socks, soak in a

solution of 2 tablespoons of borax and 1 gallon of hot water for one hour prior to laundering. Then dump the entire contents of the bucket into the washer and add detergent; wash as usual.

To revive table linens, add ½ cup of borax to your laundry along with your detergent. It will boost your detergent to remove those mystery stains and that stale odor from storage.

To easily clean cloth hats and baseball caps, put them on the top rack of the dishwasher. To avoid color fading, fill the detergent cup with borax and allow to wash up to the dry cycle. Remove the hats prior to the dry cycle and set on a pitcher or jar to dry, shaping as needed.

Make your own Queen's Power Paste by lathering Fels-Naptha® Laundry Bar Soap onto stained laundry, fabric patio cushions, etc. Then work borax into the lather, rubbing between your thumbs. Removes most difficult stains.

THE NEW GUYS

All of us have been reading about, seeing, and probably trying some of the new "oxy" cleaners and the "orange" cleaners. The market is saturated with these cleaners, each claiming to be the best and to clean "with the power of oxygen" or "the power of natural oranges."

My rule of thumb for these is to read the ingredients.

Not all of the ingredients in all of the products are safe, and not all of the products are chemical-free.

If you use an oxy cleaner on your carpet and it doesn't dissolve well and you don't remove all of it, you can end up with bleached areas on the carpet the next time it is cleaned.

Remember, there are and have been for a long time a ton of oxygen bleaches on the grocery store shelves. New does not necessarily mean better. Watch your costs. Figure out how much you are adding to washloads and how much you are using to spot-clean.

Orange cleaners work well on greasy dirt because grease removes grease, and orange cleaners have orange oil in them as well as other chemicals. Watch out for those other chemicals.

Be an informed consumer. Read the labels. Know what you are bringing home. Be aware of what you are using on your children's clothes and what chemicals they are breathing and touching. If allergies and asthma are an issue in your home, look at your cleaning chemicals and change to natural products that you make or, in some cases, can buy. You will be amazed at how well natural things can clean. Great-grandma and grandma always had a clean house and clothes, and you can, too, without spending a lot of money and using a ton of harsh chemicals.

4

WASTE NOT ...

Most of us want to be smart with our money, and what our money buys. That's why it's so frustrating to throw out those little "last-ofs." You know, the last of the dental floss, the last of the wine in the bottle, the last of the ketchup. . . . And what about all those other little doodads that are taking up space in the junk drawer, such as single chopsticks, film canisters, and the odd denture tablet from granny's last visit? Well, I believe there's more than one use for most anything, and that's what I'd like to share with you here. Did someone say *use it or lose it?*

Lifeless Lettuce: Ready for a salad but the lettuce has wilted? Just drop the droopy leaves in a bowl of cool water into which you've added a few slices of lemon or a few drops of lemon juice. Put the bowl in the fridge for about an hour, and . . . Hail, Caesar!

Red, White, and Wine: Don't throw out that little bit of wine left in the bottle—freeze it instead. You won't want to drink it, of course, but a few cubes of your favorite wine can sure add some zest to your cooking.

Don't Lose Your Marbles: Store them in an empty baby-wipes container instead. These containers—whether boxes or cylinders—are great for storing game pieces and dice, too!

Can It: Those cylindrical potato chip cans are great for holding kids' pencils and paintbrushes.

Berry Good: Keep a few plastic berry baskets in the kitchen, bathroom, and laundry room. They're great for holding soaps and sponges.

Patent Pending: Want those patent leather shoes to gleam? Rub in some petroleum jelly with a soft cloth, and buff . . . buff . . . buff . . .

Lemon Aid: Get more juice out of a lemon by putting it in the microwave for 30 seconds before squeezing.

Lost Lenses: Lost a contact lens? Cover your vacuum hose with a nylon stocking, then slowly and gently vacuum the area.

Bag It: Lost the twist tie for your bread? Try using a hair barrette instead.

Sunny-Side Up: A thin layer of plain yogurt will help take the sting out of that sunburn.

Paint by Numbers: Keep paint handy for those touch-ups by storing in a plastic detergent bottle—just make sure that you've cleaned and dried it first. The spill-proof spout makes it ideal.

For Tresses and Dresses: Run out of fabric softener before that last load is done? Use a little crème rinse instead. Vinegar is a wonder-worker, too: a cup in your rinse water makes clothes nice and soft . . . and a vinegar rinse will soften your hair, too!

Chalk It Up to Experience: A few sticks of chalk in your silverware drawer will help prevent tarnish.

Dental Floss: Makes a great thread—especially good for those hardworking buttons on heavy winter coats. (I used to live in Detroit. Trust me, I know what I'm talking about!)

Catch-up for Ketchup: Inserting a plastic straw into a slow bottle of ketchup will add some much-needed air and get that ketchup flowing.

Thermal Dynamics: Drop a few denture tablets into a thermos to keep it shiny and new. Helps get rid of coffee odors, too!

X Marks the Spot: Feel a pimple coming on? A little dab of toothpaste will dry it right up! Feel the beginnings of a cold sore? Rubbing it with raw garlic will help keep it at bay. (Works great for vampires, too.)

Eye Eye: Coffee filters are great for cleaning eyeglasses.

Close Shave: Cut yourself shaving? Dab on a little Chap Stick® to stop the bleeding.

Unhinged: A quick squirt of furniture polish will quiet that squeaky door!

Oatmeal Scrub: Don't know what to do with that little bit of oatmeal at the bottom of the bag? Make a paste with a little bit of milk and you'll have a hydrating facial scrub that will leave your skin refreshed.

Chopsticks: These make great supports for houseplants.

Film Canisters: Those little plastic containers are great for any number of jobs. Use them to keep quarters for the laundry. Take them to the gym and use them to store your jewelry. Use them to store postage stamps, sewing needles, or those little keys for your suitcases. Oh . . . apparently they're good for storing film, too!

Over the years, I have been asked some pretty interesting questions. One of the best came from a gentleman who called into a radio show to ask how to clean the tarnished silver balls on his sporran! Now, even though I am part Scottish, I didn't have a clue as to what he was asking. Fortunately for me, he was willing to explain that since there aren't any pockets in a kilt, a Scottish gentleman in full attire wears a sporran. In Queen's terms, this is a very masculine purse that is worn hanging from a strap around the waist on the front of the kilt. There are leather sporrans, semidress sporrans, and dress sporrans. (Who knew? !) Now, not all sporrans have silver balls, but those that do have the same problem that we encounter when fine silver tarnishes—it leaves a black mark on the often very expensive sporran.

My advice to men in kilts is to have some nongel toothpaste on hand to remove the tarnish. First, put several layers of paper towels over the fabric or leather and then carefully buff the silver trim with a damp cloth and toothpaste. Then rub with a clean damp cloth and buff. Another great idea is Maas® Silver Polishing Gloves. Just slip them on, rub tarnished silver gently, and you're done. One thing I never did find out is what Scottish men wear under those kilts!

5

RUST NEVER SLEEPS

Professional rust removers are readily available at grocery stores, home centers, and hardware stores. Some of them are for use only on white clothes, and others can be used on colored fabrics, too. If you are using one of these chemical products, be sure to read the directions carefully to avoid failure. If you want to remove rust from clothes with a natural, easy method and avoid chemicals, here are two ideas.

REMOVING RUST FROM CLOTHES

Apply lemon juice and let the item dry in the sun, then launder as usual. This is generally safe on all washable fabrics, but if in doubt try first in an inconspicuous place. Another method is to apply cream of tartar to the rust spot, gather up the edges of the material, and dip the spot into hot water. Let it sit for 5 minutes and then launder as usual.

TO REMOVE RUST FROM METAL

Sprinkle scouring powder on a cork, then rub the stain. Wash and rinse as usual.

TO REMOVE RUST FROM FIXTURES

Rub the rust spot with salt and lemon juice until the rust disappears. Then rinse and polish.

TO REMOVE RUST FROM THE TOILET BOWL

There are, of course, acid bowl cleaners available from grocery stores, home centers, and janitorial supply stores that will remove rust from toilets, but for an inexpensive, nontoxic way to remove rust, try this: Once a month sprinkle a layer of Tang® Breakfast Drink or lemon Kool-Aid® on the sides of the toilet and in the water, leave for an hour, brush, and flush. Repeat if necessary. (For those of you who are wondering, citric acid oxidizes the rust.)

TO REMOVE RUST FROM STAINLESS STEEL SINKS

Rub the rust spot with lighter fluid until the rust is removed, then follow up with liquid cleaner. Be careful when you do this not to work around an open flame, and be sure you have the area ventilated adequately.

TO REMOVE RUST FROM UTENSILS

This is a great, easy tip—try it the next time you're making a salad! Stick the utensils, such as knives, forks, etc., into an onion. Pull back and forth on the utensil, then let it sit there so the onion juice can do its job.

TO REMOVE RUST FROM CHROME

This tip works great on car chrome. Take a crumpled ball of aluminum foil and rub the rust spot until it disappears.

TO REMOVE RUST FROM COUNTERTOPS

This works on Formica®, plastic laminates, etc. Make a paste of cream of tartar and either lemon juice or hydrogen peroxide, apply to the rust spot, and allow to sit for about 30 minutes. Scrub with nylon-type scrubbing sponge and rinse. If necessary, repeat.

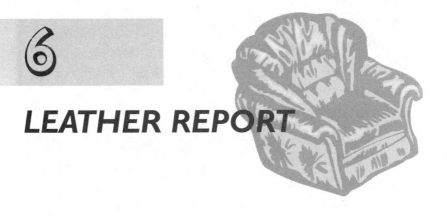

6

LEATHER REPORT

M any of us have leather furniture, car interiors, clothes, and accessories. Unfortunately, along with wearing leather and using it in our homes comes the frustration of cleaning it.

CLEANING LEATHER FURNITURE

Keep leather furniture out of direct sunlight, otherwise it may crack and dry out. You should use hide food once or twice a year to ensure that the leather remains supple. Make sure you rub it in well so that it does not come off on clothes. I like to apply it, rub it in well, let it sit for 12 hours, and then buff again before using the piece. Dust or vacuum regularly and clean with saddle soap or wipe with a damp cloth rubbed across a wet bar of glycerin soap or moisturizing facial soap, such as Dove. If the leather piece is tufted and has buttons and piping, use a soft, bristled toothbrush or paintbrush moistened and rubbed across the soap. Always dry leather with a clean, lint-free cloth.

You can keep the metal trim on your purse from tarnishing by applying a thin coat of clear nail polish. Spread a little petroleum jelly on the leather near the trim to avoid getting nail polish on the leather, and just wipe it off when the job is done.

If you have a sealed leather table or desktop, clean, polish, and seal it with paste wax once or twice a year.

LEATHER APPAREL

If you have dirty leather shoes, purses, coats, or accessories, you can treat them much the same way that you do your furniture. For cleaning purses and shoes, a damp, soft cloth rubbed across a bar of moisturizing facial soap, such as Dove, works well. You should always use care to not over-wet the article. Do not rinse after washing; instead, allow to dry naturally, then polish as usual.

WATER SPOTS

Simply run a damp sponge over the area and allow to dry. Or roll a slice of fresh bread in your hand, then rub each water spot firmly with the ball of bread.

SALT STAINS

Dab on a solution of 3 parts white vinegar to 1 part water.

INK STAINS AND SPOTS

To remove ink stains and spots from leather, apply a little cuticle remover. Dab it on the spot and rub gently with a soft cloth, wipe, and buff. You may need to allow the cuticle remover to sit for 10 minutes or so before rubbing for difficult stains. Reapply if necessary.

DARK STAINS

If you have light-colored leather furniture or apparel with dark stains on it, try wiping gently with a thin paste of lemon juice and cream of tartar. Gently massage in, then finish off with a soft, damp cloth. Be sure to rinse well and follow up with one of the cleaning methods above.

REMOVING MILDEW

To remove mildew from leather, apply a coat of petroleum jelly, allow to sit for 4–5 hours, then rub off.

MAKING HIDE FOOD

Make your own "hide food" by mixing 1 part vinegar to 2 parts linseed oil in a jar with a lid. Shake well and apply with a soft cloth, changing it frequently as it soils. Buff well so oil won't transfer to clothes. Test in an inconspicuous area before using on light-colored leather.

LEATHER CLEANER AND CONDITIONER

An incredible leather cleaner and conditioner is Leather CPR™. You can use it on all leather except for suede-type leathers. It is clear, so it leaves no residue or color that will rub off. You can use it on leather furniture, auto interiors, shoes, purses, briefcases, boots, belts, and equestrian wear, to name a few. It is called Leather CPR™ because it will

A *gentle* rub with some fine sandpaper will remove scuff marks from suede shoes.

literally save and prolong the life of your leather goods. Simply work it in with the applicator and then lightly buff. You won't believe the way it works to clean and condition. Check out www.leathercpr.com for a store location near you or to order online.

7

TAMING DUST BUNNIES WITHOUT A WHIP

Dusting is one of those thankless jobs that we all have to do. No matter how many times we do it, we still have to do it again and again. These are things that you can do to make the job easier and faster.

HOME-TREATED DUSTCLOTHS

Many dusting products are on the market that you can buy, but you can easily make your own treated dustcloths for just pennies. Here's how:

Use your favorite cleaning product to make up a bucket of hot, sudsy water. Add a couple of teaspoons of turpentine. Throw in some clean, cotton dustcloths, stir so that they get saturated, and let them soak for 8–10 hours (I usually leave them overnight). After they have soaked, wring them out and air-dry them. As soon as they are dry, they are ready to use.

Mix together two cups of hot water and one cup of lemon oil. Dip lintless cloths into the solution. Squeeze thoroughly and air-dry. Store in a covered metal can—an old coffee can works great.

LAMB'S-WOOL DUSTERS

For dusting hard-to-reach and high areas, use a good lamb's-wool duster. Do not use a feather duster; it simply shifts the dust around. A lamb's-wool duster attracts dust, is easily washed, and can be used for years. Look for these at janitorial supply stores, home centers, in mail-order catalogs, or at www.queenofclean.com.

DUST REPELLENT

To keep dust off blinds, refrigerators, and glass-top tables, mix a solution of 1 part liquid fabric softener to 4 parts water. Spray on or apply with a soft cloth and dry with a soft cloth. This will repel the dust.

DUSTING PRINTS

Use cornstarch to remove extra furniture polish and wipe off fingerprints on wood furniture. Shake a little on the surface and polish with a soft cloth.

8

FLOOR CLEANING— NOW STEP ON IT

Once you know a few basics, you can clean your floors quickly and easily—just like the pros.

CLEANING WOOD FLOORS WITH TEA

Tea is a wonderful cleaner for wood because of the tannic acid. Brew 1 quart of boiling water with 1 or 2 tea bags. Let it come to room temperature. Wring out a soft cloth to just damp and wash floor, keeping the rag clean. Do not overwet floor. This will clean the floor and cover many imperfections. Buff with a soft cloth if desired.

REPAIR SCRATCHES IN WOOD FLOORS

To fill scratches, use a crayon or combine several to match the floor. Wax crayons for wood are available at the hardware store. Work the crayon into the scratch, then heat the repair with a blow-dryer and buff with a rag. This will work the repair into the floor so well, you'll never know it's there.

AN OUNCE OF PREVENTION

MOVING DAY You can prevent scuff marks caused by moving furniture by slipping old socks over the legs of tables and chairs. (Forget to take them off and you'll have an interesting conversation piece!)

CLEAN AND WAX

Bruce® Floor Care Products (www.Florstor.com) makes a cleaner and wax in one. It comes in two colors, light and dark. If your floors are bad, you might consider trying this product before you spend the money to refinish the floors. Follow the directions on the can carefully, and allow plenty of time to do the job, working in one small area at a time.

SEALING CERAMIC TILE

Ceramic tile is not porous, but ceramic tile grout needs some maintenance. You have to seal and maintain that seal on the grout or it will start to soil and stain and you could have mold and mildew growing on it—something you definitely want to avoid!

Different types of grout sealers are available at hardware stores and home centers. Which one you choose is up to you, but here's the Queen's take on them to help you decide.

Some sealers are acrylic-based or silicon-based. Both of these form a transparent waterproof film over the grout to keep it clean and prevent the growth of mold and mildew. These are most appropriate for use on a ceramic-tile kitchen countertop or floor where spilled food is your biggest problem.

I have had success with acrylic grout sealers. They are reliable, can be used in the kitchen or bath, and form a much harder film than silicon sealers. Some sealers to look for are Eco-Lab and Cerama-Seal™. Pay attention to the directions when using any sealer.

One last sealer that I particularly love for wet, damp areas such as bath or shower and bathroom floors is

Dry-Treat (www.drytreat.com). This changes the wetability of the grout particles so that water actually beads up on the grout and doesn't get absorbed into it. That is obviously important in preventing mold and mildew. Any penetrating sealer such as this can't be washed away or eroded by the stream of water from the shower, so it lasts and lasts.

CLEANING CERAMIC TILE

Ceramic tile is not porous—you can clean it effectively with warm water. Many cleaners leave a residue on the tile surface that looks like a smeary coating. A good neutral cleaner for tile is 1 gallon warm water, 2 tablespoons of ammonia, and 1 tablespoon of borax. Never use vinegar. It is acidic and will eventually etch the grout.

Never use a sponge mop on ceramic tile. It works like a squeegee, depositing the dirty water into the grout tracks.

Sweep or vacuum floor prior to washing.

Use a rag or chamois-type mop.

Rinse mop, frequently changing the water as it becomes soiled.

If you have a gloss-finish tile, it may be necessary to dry the tile. Use a clean terry rag under your foot to do it the easy way.

DUSTING WOOD FLOORS

Use a dry dust mop to remove dust or vacuum floor, being sure not to use a vacuum with a beater bar—this can mar the floor.

CLEANING VINYL FLOORS

For cleaning vinyl floors, including no-wax floors, sheet vinyl, and linoleum:

Sweep or vacuum the floor well. Mix 1 gallon of warm water and 1 tablespoon of borax. Wring out mop or rag well after dipping in the solution and wash the floor, keeping the rag clean. No rinsing is necessary. Using borax preserves the shine on floors, even those that have been waxed.

WAXING FLOORS

When you wax a floor, it is wise to buy the wax from a janitorial store, which sells commercial products that hold up well to wear and traffic.

On a clean floor apply 2 thin coats of wax, allowing ample drying time between coats. It is imperative that the floor be clean, otherwise you will wax in the dirt.

The next time you wax, wax only the traffic area where the wax is worn off, feathering it into the other areas to blend. This eliminates wax buildup around the edges of the room.

Purchase a wax-stripping product from your local janitorial supply store. It is more efficient than ammonia and also reasonably priced.

THE MIRACLE OF MICROFIBER . . . OR IS IT?

Microfiber cloths and mops clean without chemicals—just water and the cloth or mop. Do these products work? Well . . . yes and no. The old adage *you get what you pay for* certainly holds true in the microfiber business. If you are purchasing these cloths dirt cheap, you are wasting your money. If they do not contain thousands of fibers, they won't clean as they should. Here's the dirty lowdown on the very best.

Euronet USA makes the ACT Natural® Mop. A dry/wet mop with a telescoping handle, this miracle cleans vinyl, ceramic, wood—any hard flooring—beautifully with nothing but water. Just wring the mop out in water, stick it to the Velcro® pad, and go! Machine wash. Check out www.actnatural.net, www.euronetusa.com, or call 888-638-2882.

WASH-AND-TOSS MOPS

We've all seen and many of you have tried the new mops with the wash-and-toss sheets that are replaceable. These come in kits and some even have dispensers for cleaning so-lution.

Do they work?

- First of all, the handle is too short to mop com-fortably. A mop handle should be at shoulder height.

- The commercials seem to imply that you can at-tach one sheet to the mop head and mop your entire house. Would you use your sponge, microfiber, or rag mop to mop your entire house without rinsing it? Of course not. This means that in washing a 10-by-12 floor with this type of mop, you should probably change the replacement cloth at least four times. That starts to cost a lot of money. If you are not changing the cloth, you are mopping with a dirty mop and spreading the dirt around rather than removing it. This means that your floors and grout will eventually become heavily soiled.

- Of course the manufacturers of the various mops in this category count on you to return to the store over and over for refills and for mop kits to re-place worn-out and broken ones.

- If you use this type of floor-cleaning system, make sure you are changing the throwaway pad as often as you would rinse a regular mop.

- I have heard of people putting dryer fabric-softener sheets and paper towels on the mop heads to save money. Don't do that. They don't begin to clean properly and can leave fine scratches in wood floors. Fabric-softener sheets can also make floors slippery.

As for the Queen, I will stick with my ACT Natural® Mop with its two-year warranty, adjustable handle, and machine-washable mop head.

9

THE QUEEN'S ROYAL CARPET TREATMENT

Carpet is one of the most expensive investments you will make in your home. With proper knowledge about choosing a good-quality carpet that fits your lifestyle, and cleaning and stain-removal guidelines, your carpet will give you many years of enjoyment and quality wear.

KNOW YOUR CARPET

Most residential carpet is made from one of four fibers: nylon, polyester, olefin, or wool (or a combination). All of these fibers can make great carpet, although nylon is one of the most cost-effective and durable. Here are some other things to be aware of when making that important purchase.

Face Weight is a commonsense measurement that you should be aware of when purchasing carpet. The key to remember: More fibers are almost always better.

Fiber Density is a measurement of how closely packed carpet fibers are to each other. Carpets with high density tend to look better longer and will give carpet a soft feeling when walked upon.

Carpet Fiber Twist is important to be aware of, especially with cut-pile types of carpet. Fibers that have more twists per linear inch usually make more durable carpeting.

Carpet Padding is absolutely critical to good carpet performance. Too much or too little can cause premature failure in many carpets. The best pads, believe it or not, are thin and firm. Avoid pads thicker than $\frac{7}{16}$ inch.

CLEANING CARPET

Many people ask me how to go about hiring a firm to clean carpeting. Listed below are some general guidelines. Always call more than one company, looking for comparable pricing. Ask each company the same set of questions, and remember, word of mouth is one of your best allies. Ask your neighbors, your friends, the people you work with, which companies they have used and how satisfied they were.

QUESTIONS TO ASK

Cost per Square Foot or Room

Find out if there is a square-footage limitation per room and if your room sizes fit within the limitation. Remember to ask about hallways, walk-in closets, and bathrooms. They may count as a whole room when companies offer room pricing. If the cost is figured by square foot, measure the length and width of your rooms and multiply length by width to achieve the square footage. Add the total square footage of all of your rooms and multiply by the cost per square foot. This should give you an accurate price.

Find Out What Method of Cleaning Is Used

Steam cleaning or extraction is the preferable way to clean. Ask if the company uses a "truck-mounted unit." A portable cleaner will not generate the same powerful extraction process that a truck unit will.

Do They Clean with Hot or Cold Water?

Cold water will not remove stubborn, greasy soil. A truck-mounted cleaning system should hook up to your cold water, usually at an outside tap, and heat the water as it flows through the truck.

Is the Company Insured?

If they damage your furniture while moving it or bang into a wall, you want to be sure they can cover the cost of the repair.

Ask About Experience

Be sure you are hiring trained professionals who do this for a living.

Remember the Investment

Again, carpet is one of your most expensive investments, so treat it with the care it deserves and it will last much longer and look better.

BEFORE CLEANING CARPETS

- Pick up all small items from carpets.
- Remove all items from furniture to be moved.
- When possible, remove dining chairs and other small, light pieces of furniture.

- Pick up all small area rugs.
- Remove things from the floor of the closet if it will be cleaned.
- Remove anything from under beds if they are to be moved.
- Open as many windows as possible, if weather permits.
- If house is not left open, turn on the air conditioner or heat, whichever is appropriate.
- If possible, set fans so they blow across the carpet.
- Wash the soles of the shoes or slippers that you will be wearing on the damp carpet, otherwise dirt from the soles will be transferred to the carpet.
- Do not move furniture back until carpet is completely dry.

AFTER CARPETS ARE CLEANED

BEWARE of slippery linoleum and other hard floors when stepping from damp carpet.

- Do not put towels or sheets or newspapers on the carpet.
- If you have had the carpet treated with carpet protector, you will need to allow extra drying time.
- Vacuum carpet thoroughly after it is dry with a clean vacuum.

SPOTTING GUIDE

The number one rule of spot removal on carpet is to always keep several bottles of club soda on hand to use on spills on any kind of carpet. If you spill, follow this advice:

- Blot up as much moisture as you can—laying old towels over the spill and standing on them is a great way to start.
- Scrape up any solids.
- Pour club soda on the spill. Don't be afraid to really pour it on. The carbonation in the soda will "bubble up" the spill so that you can blot it up. Again, cover the spot with clean, light-colored towels or rags and stand on them. This will really help to absorb the spill. Continue to pour and absorb until all color from the stain has been blotted up and the towel is coming up clean.
- Follow up with a good carpet stain remover.
- When you spot-clean carpet, never rub, as it will only spread the stain and will cause abrasion to the carpet fibers.
- This is a good general cleaning method for most spills and definitely will not cause any damage.

Red Pop, Kool-Aid®

Grab the club soda fast and follow the above method. If the stain is old, still try the club soda—it will help lighten the stain. After using your carpet spotter, if the spot is still present, saturate with hydrogen peroxide or undiluted lemon juice. Wait 15 minutes and blot. Continue to apply and check your progress, just to be sure you aren't lightening the carpet.

Red Wine

Grab the white wine and pour it on or saturate with salt and follow with the club soda and carpet spotter.

Nail Polish

Blot up as much polish as possible with a tissue or anything handy. Then test the effect of nonoily nail polish remover on an inconspicuous part of the carpet. If there are no ill effects to the carpet pile, apply the nail polish remover with an eyedropper or a nonsilver spoon, blotting immediately after each application. Always use nonoily polish remover. If regular nail polish remover does not work, buy straight acetone at a beauty supply house, pretest again, and apply as directed above. Once you have removed as much as possible (have patience), follow with a good carpet stain remover, applied according to the directions. If color staining remains, apply hydrogen peroxide to bleach or lighten the stain.

Mud

Cover wet mud with salt or baking soda and let dry thoroughly before touching. Once it is dry, vacuum it using the attachment hose to concentrate the suction on the mud. Use a good carpet spotter, following the directions, to complete the process. For red dirt or mud, use a rust remover such as Whink® or Rust Magic® to remove any color residue. Make sure you test the rust remover in a small area first.

Coffee and Tea

The best defense is a good offense when you spill coffee. First, act as quickly as possible. Hot coffee is the equivalent of brown dye. Blot up all of the spill that you can and immediately apply club soda. If you don't have club soda (shame on you), use plain cold water. Really pour it on and blot, blot, blot. Follow with a good-quality carpet spotter. If a stain remains, you can attempt to remove it by pouring on hydrogen peroxide, waiting 15 minutes, and then blotting. If it is lightening the stain,

PALACE PENNYSAVERS

USE SHAVING CREAM The great instant spot remover! If you have a spill and have no carpet spotter available, grab the shaving cream. It is particularly effective on makeup, lipstick, coffee, and tea. Work it into the spot well and rinse with either cold water or club soda.

continue, and as a final step, rinse with cold water or club soda.

GUIDE TO SPECIAL SPOTS

Spots Such as Tar and Mustard

Work glycerin (available at drugstores in the hand cream section) into the spot. Let it sit 30–60 minutes. Working carefully with paper towels, use a lifting motion to remove the spot. This may require multiple treatments. Follow with a good spotter.

Removing Indentations in Carpet

Lay ice cubes in the indentations caused by furniture. Be sure to cover all of the indented area. Leave overnight and then fluff the nap with the tines of a fork the next day.

Candle Wax

Put ice in a plastic bag and lay over the wax, allowing it to freeze. Chip off all wax that you can. Next, lay brown paper over the wax (a grocery bag works great; use the area without the writing) and press with a medium/hot iron. Move the paper as it absorbs so that you don't redeposit the wax on the carpet. Have patience and continue as long as any wax shows up on the bag. Next, apply a good carpet stain remover.

Soot

Sprinkle with salt and wait at least 2 hours and then vacuum, using the attachment hose to concentrate the suction. Spot with a good spotter.

Gum

Freeze with ice in a bag and chip off all that you can. Work a little petroleum jelly into the remaining residue and roll the gum into it. Scrape up and follow with a good spotter.

Glue

Try saturating glue with undiluted white vinegar. Working with an upward motion, work it out of the fibers and spot with a good spotter. For rubber cement, use the method above for gum.

Ink

Spray on hair spray or blot with rubbing alcohol. For heavy spots, try denatured alcohol. Blot well and follow with a spotter.

Armed for Battle

Always keep a good carpet-spotting product on hand! I have found two incredible products that remove not only fresh red stains but also old ones. Wine Away® Red Wine

Stain Remover will work effectively on such things as red wine, coffee, tea, and cranberry juice. Red Erase™ will work on kid stains, such as red pop, and even red-colored children's medicines. They are totally nontoxic and work on carpet, upholstery, car seats, and almost any fabric. Call 888-WINEAWAY for a purchase location for both products near you.

10

TODAY'S WOOD— TOMORROW'S HEIRLOOMS

Wood furniture in a home is a big investment. Properly cared for, it will last and keep its new appearance for years, eventually to be called "antique" by our grandchildren and great-grandchildren. Here are some tips to keep your furniture looking great, some tips on fixing problems that arise, plus the recipe for making your own furniture polish.

MAKING YOUR OWN FURNITURE POLISH

You can make several great furniture polishes at home with ease. The general rule for homemade polish is to rub it in with a soft cloth and wipe it off and buff with another clean, soft cloth.

Combine ¼ cup white vinegar and 1 cup olive oil in a clean container. Shake before each use.

Combine 1 cup of mineral oil and 3 drops of lemon extract. Shake before each use.

Grate 2 ounces of beeswax (available at drugstores) into a jar and cover it with 5 ounces of natural turpentine. Shake occasionally until dissolved or stand in a bowl of hot water. Apply to furniture with a soft cloth (just a small amount is all that is needed) and buff with a clean, soft cloth. If it becomes hard over time, set it in a bowl of hot water. This formula seems to work especially well on unvarnished furniture.

WATER MARKS, HEAT SCARS, AND WHITE RINGS

Massage mayonnaise into the marks and leave it on overnight. The next morning, wipe off the mayonnaise and the marks should be gone. You can also use petroleum jelly, butter, or margarine. If you have a really stubborn spot, mix cigarette ashes or rottenstone (available at the hardware store) with the mayonnaise and repeat the above procedure.

Nongel white toothpaste is also effective in removing

white water rings. Dab toothpaste on a damp cloth and gently massage the ring in a circular motion until it's gone. Wipe and buff with a soft cloth. Apply furniture polish if necessary.

REMOVE OLD POLISH AND DIRT

Put 2 tea bags in a pot with 1 quart of water and bring it to a boil. Cool to room temperature. Dip a soft cloth in the solution, wring it until it is just damp, and wipe furniture with it. Buff it dry with a soft cloth, then decide if it requires polish.

RESTORING DRIED-OUT FURNITURE

Dab petroleum jelly on a soft cloth and polish to help feed and restore dry wood. You will be amazed to see the wood grain and natural luster appear.

AN OUNCE OF PREVENTION

STICKING DRAWERS Prevent drawers from sticking by rubbing them with bar soap.

CLEANING VERY DIRTY WOOD FURNITURE

Mix a solution of 1 quart warm water and 3–4 drops of dishwashing liquid. Wash the furniture with a soft cloth wrung out until it is damp, rinse, and buff dry.

COVERING SCRATCHES

To cover scratches on wood furniture, use a crayon the color of the wood. Apply to the scratched area, heat with a blow-dryer, and buff the crayon into the scratch with a soft cloth.

For darker woods, rub the meat of a pecan or walnut into the scratch and buff well.

To cover scratches on mahogany or cherrywood, use iodine.

ERASE SCUFF MARKS

No matter how careful you and your family are, scuff marks from shoes and from your vacuum cleaner are sure to wind up on the base of your wooden furniture. To remove these marks, first rub the area with a high-quality furniture oil, such as lemon or almond oil. Then lightly rub the area with 0000 (fine) steel wool and wipe off the excess oil and residue with a soft cloth.

POTPOURRI KILLS

Believe it or not, the ever-popular potpourri will eat the finish off furniture even if it's still in the plastic bag it came in! Don't place the bag of potpourri directly on the wood finish, and when using it, place it in an appropriate-size container to prevent it from falling onto the wood surface.

GOT SQUEAKY DRAWERS?

When wood rubs on wood, you will need something to keep the two surfaces lubricated and running smoothly. The best thing to do is put a coat of good-quality paste wax on the bottom of the drawer and on the wood it rides on. Even if the drawer is sticking, this should help.

REMOVING STICKERS FROM WOOD

To remove a price tag, identifying label, or decal from wood, pull up as much of the sticker as possible, then dip a cloth in vegetable oil or baby oil and gently scrub the area until the sticker and adhesive are gone. Finish by buffing well with a soft cloth.

11

WALL TO WALL

Wall-washing can actually be easy if you have the right equipment and do it the right way. Here are some tips for spotting, removing marks, and washing walls.

HAVE ALL THE RIGHT STUFF

When you are ready to wash walls, be sure you gather up the right things to do the job quickly and easily. Get things together before you start and have the furniture moved away from the walls so that the washing will flow smoothly. Do it like a professional. Here is a list of the things you should have:

    2 buckets
    Natural sponge (not one of those awful nylon ones)
    Baking soda and a soft rag
    Art gum eraser
    Drop cloths
    Ladder
    Ingredients for cleaning solution of your choice
    2 strips of washcloth or terry rags and 2 rubber
        bands

REMOVING MARKS

The first thing you want to try to do is erase the marks on the wall. Use an art gum eraser that you keep on hand for

QUICK TIP

Use a drop cloth on the floor around the area you will be washing—it will save you time and mess in the long run. A fabric drop cloth is preferable to plastic, as it absorbs and isn't slippery when wet. Before you start to wash, wrap a strip of washcloth or Turkish toweling around your wrist several times and secure with rubber bands. This will keep drips from running down your arms when you are working with your arms above your head.

this purpose and erase just the mark. This works on many types of marks. If you still have some stubborn spots, use a little baking soda on the corner of a white rag and rub gently, doing just the mark. Nongel toothpaste also is a good spot remover; use it on a cloth over the tip of your finger.

CRAYON MARKS

If you have kids, you have probably had crayon on the wall. To remove crayon easily, spray with WD-40® Lubricant and wipe crayon away with a paper towel. Follow up with a soft cloth and a solution of hot water and a little dishwashing liquid, washing in a circular motion.

INK AND MARKER MARKS

To remove ink or Magic Marker®, use hair spray (the cheaper the better), rubbing alcohol, or for really tough spots, denatured alcohol from the hardware store. Always spot carefully, trying to do just the spot.

GREAT WALL-WASHING SOLUTIONS

Try one of these wall-washing solutions:

- 1 gallon warm water, ½ cup ammonia, ¼ cup white vinegar, and ¼ cup washing soda

- 1 gallon warm water, 1 cup ammonia, and 1 teaspoon mild dishwashing liquid

For really professional results, rinse the walls with clear water after washing with either of these solutions. If you choose not to rinse, then be sure to change the cleaning solution frequently as it becomes soiled.

All-Purpose Cleaner

7 cups warm water
½ cup baking soda
½ cup clear ammonia

Combine ammonia, baking soda, and 1 cup of warm water in a half-gallon jug. Cap and shake until thoroughly mixed. Add remaining water and label the container.

To use: Pour ½ cup of the mixture into 1½ gallons of hot water. When using on a delicate surface like wallpaper, test in an inconspicuous area first.

WHERE TO START

You have the wall free of marks, your drop cloths are in place, your wrists are wrapped for drips, and you have your washing solution ready. Now wet your natural sponge (available at janitorial supply stores, home centers, and hardware stores). Don't skimp and use a nylon sponge or a rag; it will drag as you wash and take you twice as long. A natural sponge has thousands of "scrubbing fingers" and will get the job done fast, easy, and right. Begin washing at the bottom of the wall and work up, doing the ceiling last. Drips of water are much easier to wipe off a clean wall and won't leave marks like they do on a soiled wall.

DON'T STOP!

Once you start on a wall, don't stop in the middle. Complete one full wall or the full ceiling before you take a break. If you stop in the middle of a wall or ceiling, you will have "tide marks" where you stop and start again.

KEEPING WALLS CLEAN

You can make your own brushing tool to use between washing, to dust down the walls. Tie a clean dustcloth loosely around a broom head and use to dust ceilings thoroughly from time to time and to dust down walls. Give the broom a shake now and then as you are working to remove dust.

GREASE SPOTS ON WALLPAPER

Make a paste of cornstarch and water and apply to the grease spot. Allow it to dry, then brush or vacuum it off.

Apply a double fold of brown paper (a grocery bag works well, but don't use the part with the writing on it) and press over the grease spot with a warm iron. This may require several efforts. This method also works well on candle wax. Follow up with a little hair spray or alcohol. Always test in an inconspicuous area before proceeding.

REMOVING CRAYON FROM WALLPAPER

Rub lightly with a dry soap-filled steel-wool pad. Do this very gently. You can also try rubbing with baking soda on a damp cloth. On vinyl paper, try using a little silver polish.

SMUDGES, MARKS, AND MYSTERY STAINS ON WALLPAPER

Erase with an art gum eraser.

To remove marks from nonwashable paper: Rub a scrunched-up piece of white bread over the marks. Rub very gently. You may need to repeat this a few times before you make progress.

WASHING WALLPAPER

Wash vinyl and washable papers with one of the mild wall-washing solutions in this chapter.

CLOTH WALL COVERINGS

To clean grass-cloth, burlap, or cloth wall coverings, vacuum with the soft duster brush on the vacuum. Do this regularly to maintain the appearance.

WOOD PANELING

Clean wood paneling following the suggestions in the chapter on wood-floor cleaning.

Some of my best questions come from listeners of KEZ 99.9 radio in Phoenix. Recently, a woman called in to ask how to remove "globber" from her walls. She said it was on the walls, floors, cabinets—pretty much everywhere. Well, do I have to tell you that the hosts and I were all at a loss as to what globber was? So, with some hesitation (and a finger on the cut button, I can tell you), I asked. The answer? It's that combination of slobber and guck that bulldogs and pugs seem to get all over the place as they shake their heads from side to side and flap those big lips. Not a pretty picture—but easily solved. Make a lather of Fels-Naptha® Laundry Bar Soap on a light-colored rag and wash in a circular motion. Rinse well and pet the dog.

12

SITTING DOWN ON THE JOB— UPHOLSTERY CLEANING MADE EASY

This chapter will give you all the information you need to choose upholstered furniture wisely, spot-clean it, handle emergency spills, and clean it thoroughly.

One of the first things everyone should know about upholstery is that there are different cleaning methods for different types of fabric. There is a simple way to check to see how the furniture you have now should be cleaned and, even more important, how a new piece should be cleaned.

This will help you make good decisions on wearability and cleanability before you get the piece home.

CLEANING CODES AND WHAT THEY MEAN

Upholstery is supposed to be marked with a code that allows the consumer to know in advance what type of cleaning the manufacturer recommends for that particular piece of furniture. These instructions, known as cleaning codes, are generally found under the seat cushions on the platform of the furniture (the part that the cushions sit on). I will discuss each cleaning code individually below. If you do not find the code under the seat cushions, check all tags for instructions and never buy any upholstered furniture without knowing how it can be cleaned. This information is essential.

W

If you find a W on your furniture, it means that it can be cleaned with water. This would mean that you could rent an extraction carpet and upholstery cleaning machine from the home center or hardware store or use one that you have purchased to clean the fabric. You can also use water in spotting spills. This is the most durable and cleanable fabric you can buy. It is ideal for dining chairs, family room furniture, anything that gets heavy use or where spills might occur frequently.

S

If you find an *S* on your furniture, it means that it must be cleaned with cleaning solvents (dry-clean only) and you cannot apply water to it. This would eliminate spot-cleaning with water-based products. Dry-clean-only fabrics are generally not as durable and also do not clean as well. If you have a piece with this code, do not allow it to become heavily soiled before calling in a professional cleaner or you will be disappointed with the results. If you need to spot-clean a dry-clean-only fabric, try using a good spotter. Test it first in an inconspicuous spot to be sure it doesn't damage the fabric. Apply with a clean, light-colored cloth and blot continuously. Once you have removed the spot, use a blow-dryer to dry the spot quickly so it doesn't leave a noticeable ring on the fabric.

S/W

This code means a combination of solvents and water can be used to clean the upholstery. It does not appear on many pieces. It is best left to the professionals to clean this. Use furniture with this code in low-use areas.

X

This code does not appear on furniture as much anymore, but it does appear frequently on fabric blinds and shades. It means that the item is not cleanable and is a vacuum-only piece. Beware!

DON'T UNDRESS YOUR FURNITURE

Many people have asked me about taking the covers off the foam cushions and washing them in the washing machine—DON'T DO IT! The zippers are in the backs of cushions only so that the foam cushions may be changed by a professional if necessary. If you remove the cushion covers and wash them, they may shrink and not fit back on the foam correctly; no matter what, it is virtually impossible to get them back on the foam forms evenly and correctly. Plus, they will be noticeably cleaner than the rest of the sofa and will fade and wear out more quickly.

PALACE PENNYSAVERS

CANDLE OPERA Candles will last longer if they're stored in the refrigerator. Less drips, too!

SPOT-CLEANING

If you need to spot-clean a cushion, unzip the zipper and put a pad of paper towels or a folded white rag between the foam and the cushion covering. Apply your spotter, carefully following the directions. Try not to rub the area, as it causes abrasion on the fabric surface—BLOT—BLOT—BLOT. Remember, whatever spotting method you choose, always first do a test area where it won't show.

I have had success using club soda as a spotter. Follow the same directions as above.

CANDLE WAX MEETS UPHOLSTERY

If you unfortunately spill candle wax on your upholstery, don't despair. First, put a large quantity of ice in a plastic bag and lay it on the wax long enough to freeze the wax. Remove the ice and immediately chip up any wax that you can.

Next, take a brown grocery bag and, using only the part without writing, lay it over the wax. You can also use an old fairly wet cloth. This will ruin the cloth, so be sure it's a throwaway. Using a medium/hot iron, press over the wax, allowing it to absorb into the paper bag. Move the bag continuously to a clean area. Once you have absorbed as much of the wax as possible, use a good spotter to spot-clean the area, remembering to use a blow-dryer to dry the spot when you are done.

If any staining remains, use 3 percent hydrogen peroxide from the drugstore applied with a spoon to bleach out the wax color. Apply peroxide, wait 15 minutes, and blot, continuing until the color from the wax is gone.

13

METICULOUS MARBLE— LEAVE NO STONE UNTURNED

Bathroom and kitchen countertops are usually synthetic (cultured marble). However, marble used in living room and other furniture is usually the genuine article, as is marble flooring. Seal it with a stone sealer when it is new because it is very susceptible to stains, and wipe up spills quickly because marble absorbs moisture. It can also easily be scratched by grit. Be realistic about your expectations when you have real marble flooring or furniture. It will probably not maintain its showroom shine and some scratching cannot be avoided.

Clean marble regularly by sweeping it first and then using a soft cloth or sponge with a solution of mild liquid soap and warm water to wash it. Do not overwet the marble; instead use a damp cloth or sponge and keep the cloth or sponge clean as you work. It is a good idea to rinse marble and dry it with a soft cloth after washing. Do not use acidic products, such as vinegar or lemon juice, as they will etch the marble. Other things to avoid are scourers and solvent-based cleaners.

As you are washing, if you find spots that are not responding to the washing solution, sprinkle on a little 20 Mule Team® Borax or baking powder and rub with the damp cloth or sponge. You can also use a commercial marble polish available at hardware stores and home centers.

Bathroom and kitchen marble can be cleaned with 1 part liquid fabric softener to 2 parts warm water. Clean thoroughly and polish with a soft cloth.

If you have old marble that you are trying to clean and restore, this old-fashioned recipe has been around for years, but it still works. It is effective on heavily soiled surfaces and for stains.

Cut up 3–4 bars of Ivory® Soap and dissolve them in hot water until you have a thick, gelatin-like syrup (you can grate them if you want). Paint

When you are spotting marble, remember that warming it first with a blow-dryer will open the pores and make it easier to remove the stain.

To restore the shine to marble, rub with a cloth dampened with turpentine and then buff well. Dispose of the cloths outside in the trash when you are done.

this on the marble and let it sit for about a week. If the thick syrup starts to dry, simply add some additional water to the mix or add more of the solution. At the end of the week, rinse off the Ivory® Soap solution, rinsing several times, and dry with a soft cloth.

Now let's talk about other stains.

GREASE STAINS

Grease stains are usually circular in shape and often dark in the center, where the initial grease landed and then spread. Wash the circular area with clear ammonia and rinse extremely well. If this does not work, try saturating the stained area with 3 percent hydrogen peroxide and then working in powdered whiting (available at hardware and home centers in the paint department). Cover the area with plastic wrap and tape it down with masking tape. Let sit for 15 minutes, then rinse well. Repeat as necessary. Buff and then polish and reseal the area.

RUST STAINS

Use a mixture of commercial rust remover and powdered whiting to remove rust. Follow the directions for grease stains. Once the rust is removed, rinse well and rub with a dry cloth. This method also works for tea and coffee stains.

WATER STAINS

A wet glass will leave a ring on marble. To remove it, apply 3 percent hydrogen peroxide with an eyedropper or spoon, then add a drop or two of clear ammonia. After 30 minutes, wipe the area with a paper towel, rinse, and dry.

WINE

For white wine stains, saturate the area with 3 percent hydrogen peroxide. Let sit 15 minutes or so and then rinse and dry. For red wine, use Wine Away® Red Wine Stain Remover as directed on the container.

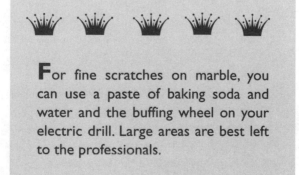

For fine scratches on marble, you can use a paste of baking soda and water and the buffing wheel on your electric drill. Large areas are best left to the professionals.

MYSTERY STAINS

Many times you will find a stain on marble and have no idea what it is. For those stains, combine 3 percent hydrogen peroxide and some cream of tartar and rub with a soft cloth until the stain is removed. For tougher stains, massage with some nongel toothpaste and a soft cloth, then follow with the hydrogen peroxide and cream of tartar treatment again.

14

PET PROJECTS

o your pets have accidents in the house? Did you have a pet-sitter while you were on a trip and the cat didn't use the litterbox and the dog didn't go outside? Do you know what to do when the cat leaves you a hair ball surprise on the carpet or the spaghetti didn't agree with the dog? Help is on the way! Here's all the information you need to clean up pet accidents and keep them from happening again.

PET ODOR

Pet odor caused by urine or feces is one of the toughest deodorizing problems you will face. The stain from the problem is only a small part of the dilemma. Unless you completely deodorize the area where the pet accident occurred, the animal, especially cats, will return to the spot and resoil it.

Pet odor is a protein-based problem and cannot be eliminated by normal spotting procedures. Do not be fooled into believing that you can spray on a deodorizer and the odor will magically disappear. It won't happen, and you will have wasted time and money on a product that doesn't work. Now let's get to the basics of pet odor removal.

FIRST, REMOVE AND BLOT

You must remove any solid waste from the area and blot up any liquid residue using a heavy pad, paper towels, or old, disposable rags. Lay this pad on the carpet and stand on it to absorb as much liquid as possible.

STEP TWO, TREAT

Pour on club soda. The carbonation will bubble the remaining soil to the surface, and the salts in the club soda will keep it from staining. Now blot firmly again with paper towels. Do this procedure 3 or 4 times, and the last time lay a thick layer of paper towels down and then stand on them to remove all the moisture you can. Continue to do this until you have removed all the moisture you possibly can. Allow to air-dry. To speed drying, use a fan.

STEP THREE

Treat the area with your favorite carpet spotter. If you don't have carpet spotter handy, mix a mild solution of white vinegar and water (⅓ cup white vinegar in a 1-quart bottle filled with cool water) in a spray bottle and spray onto the pet stains to help remove the discoloration. Rinse with clear water and blot.

If you still have staining, combine ½ cup of hydrogen peroxide with 1 teaspoon of ammonia and saturate the stained area. Allow to sit for 30 minutes and then blot. Continue to treat until all the stain is removed or the solution has removed all that can possibly be removed.

STEP FOUR

Once the area is totally dry, apply a thin layer of ODORZ-OUT®. Use this product dry. Allow it to sit for 24 hours and then vacuum up. Continue to apply and vacuum until the ODORZOUT® has absorbed all of the odor. ODORZ-OUT® is 100 percent safe and natural, so it will not harm kids or pets even if they walk through it.

OOPS! THE CARPET CHANGED COLOR

Urine spots may change the carpet color. The carpet may be lightened or bleached. Many times this is not obvious until the carpet is cleaned the first time after the accident. It is more common when the stain has not been treated in an appropriate manner. If this happens, try sponging the area with a mild ammonia solution. This will sometimes return the carpet to its original color or at least make it less noticeable.

PET ACCIDENTS ON UPHOLSTERED FURNITURE

When pets have accidents on upholstered furniture, you must first be sure that the fabric can be cleaned and treated with water. Check the platform of the sofa or chair under the cushion to determine the cleaning code. It should

Anyone who loves cats knows how difficult it is to get them to swallow pills. Here's a great trick: Blow gently into kitty's face once she has the pill in her mouth. The breeze will cause her to close her eyes, and also to swallow!

be listed on a tag. *W* indicates that the piece can be cleaned with water, so it can be treated as described on page 92. Clean the area using a good-quality upholstery spotting product. If the code is an *S*, this means solvent must be used in the cleaning process and this must be done by a professional. Do not apply an enzyme product or spotter. Call a professional. In this instance, the foam in the cushion may require replacing after cleaning.

If a pet urinates on a mattress, use a steam extraction machine to remove all the urine you can. Continue to clean with the extraction machine, and try to get out

The dachshund is one of the oldest dog breeds in history (dating back to ancient Egypt). The name comes from one of its earliest uses—hunting badgers. In German, *Dachs* means "badger," *Hund* is "hound."

all the moisture. Stand the mattress on edge to thoroughly dry—at least 12 hours. Once dry, if odor is present, apply ODORZOUT® to eliminate the smell.

WHEN THE CAT LEAVES YOU A HAIR BALL OR THE SPAGHETTI DOESN'T AGREE WITH THE DOG

If you have pets, you know what it's like when your cat or dog suffers a digestive upset. You hear the problem begin and run to move the dog or cat off the carpet (which seems to be their favorite place to leave "gifts"), but you're too late and faced with a mess to clean up.

First, resist the temptation to wipe up the mess. If there are solids that can be picked up with a paper towel, do so, but do not smear the accident into the carpet. Trying to wipe it up immediately will only make the mess worse. Instead, sprinkle a heavy coating of baking soda on the area and allow it to dry. The baking soda will absorb moisture and digestive acids. Once the area is dry, remove with paper towels or vacuum the area, removing all of the mess that will come up. Vacuum thoroughly to remove the baking soda. Then and only then should you grab the rag and the cleaner. Use your favorite carpet spotter, following the directions carefully. Remember to blot rather than rub.

French poodles did not originate in France. Poodles were originally used as hunting dogs in other parts of Europe. The dogs' thick coats were a hindrance in water and thick brush, so hunters sheared the hindquarters, with cuffs left around the ankles and hips to protect against rheumatism.

If any discoloration remains after cleaning, try applying either undiluted lemon juice or hydrogen peroxide from the drugstore. Let it soak on the stain for 15 minutes and then blot. If the spot is still visible, apply again, watching carefully to be sure that there are no changes in carpet color. If you need a more aggressive treatment, mix lemon juice and cream of tartar into a thin paste. Apply to the spot, let dry, then vacuum up. When done with any of these procedures, rinse the carpet with cool water.

REMOVING PET HAIR FROM FABRIC

Sometimes the vacuum cleaner isn't enough to remove pet hair from upholstered furniture. In this case, try one of the following methods:

- Dampen a sponge and wipe over the furniture, rinsing the sponge as necessary.
- Wipe down with your hands while wearing rubber gloves.
- Wrap Scotch® tape around hands and wipe, changing as needed.
- Wipe with dampened body-washing puff.
- Wipe with a used dryer fabric-softener sheet.

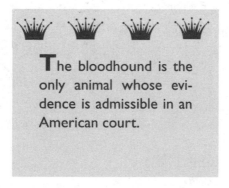

The bloodhound is the only animal whose evidence is admissible in an American court.

KEEPING CATS FROM DIGGING IN YOUR HOUSE PLANTS

To keep your cat from digging in indoor flowerpots, place a cotton ball dipped in oil of cloves just below the soil line.

If your pet is eating your house plants, here's a great product to try. It's called Bitter Apple and is simply sprayed on the plant leaves. It won't hurt the plant or your pet. Its bitter taste will immediately stop the pet from chewing on the plant. Try your local pet store.

KEEPING FLEAS OUT OF DOGHOUSES

To deter fleas, sprinkle salt in the crevices of the dog-house.

PALACE PENNYSAVERS

SAGE ADVICE Protect your dogs and cats from fleas—and protect yourself from high vet bills!—by sprinkling a little sage in their food. A little canned pumpkin will prevent constipation in kitties, too!

CARING FOR CAGED BIRDS

One of the best ways to keep your bird healthy is to keep its cage as clean as possible. Keep the cage clean by lining the slide-out bottom with newspaper (black-and-white only; don't use the comics, as colored ink can be toxic). Replace this lining every day. If your cage has a rack separating the bird from the cage bottom, you can also use corn-type litter from the pet store. This is clean and easy to use and controls odor, too.

You should also wash your bird's food and water bowls daily in hot, sudsy water and rinse them thoroughly in hot water. Dry the food dish completely before you place new food in it, because damp food quickly breeds life-threatening molds and bacteria.

Once a week, disinfect the birdcage by washing the slide-out tray in a chlorine solution (follow bottle directions carefully) and rinsing thoroughly with warm water. Make sure your bird is in another room of the house or in another cage while you do this. Don't leave it unattended if you have a cat in the house. You know how they love to play! Now you need to clean the rest of the cage. If it's relatively small, you may want to place the whole thing in the bathtub and wash the plastic parts in the chlorine solution, then rinse thoroughly in warm water. Chlorine can pit or discolor brass and other metals, so consider washing these metal parts with hot, soapy water instead, then rinse thoroughly so that no residue remains. Remember, birds should never be exposed to chemicals, so rinsing is vital. For stubborn areas, a paste of baking soda and water makes a quick and safe cleaner.

If your bird's cage is too large to place in the tub, clean it where it stands. Use a sponge and a bucket of hot, soapy water to wash it down. Rinse with a clean sponge soaked in fresh water. For extra disinfecting you can dampen paper towels with rubbing alcohol and give the entire cage a wipe-down, then rinse thoroughly again afterward. You can also take the cage outside and wash it well with hot, soapy water, then rinse thoroughly with the hose. Of course, your bird should be in a spare cage while you are doing this.

15

KIDDING AROUND

Kids are life's reward and add great joy to our lives. They also test all of our patience and cleaning skills. If you have children, large or small, or you have grand-children, you need to memorize this chapter, or at least know where this book is at all times!

BABY SHOES

To make baby shoes easy to polish, rub them with the cut side of a raw potato or some rubbing alcohol prior to polishing. After polishing, spray with hair spray to keep the polish from rubbing off so easily. Put a little clear nail polish on the areas that are always scuffed and the shoes won't wear as much in those areas.

BATH HELPERS

Put small slivers of mild soap into the open end of a small sock and tie shut, or make a small slit in a small sponge and insert soap. These won't slip out of small hands (or yours when washing the baby).

For a great safe way to bathe a toddler, put a plastic laundry basket with mesh openings in the tub and put the child in it. It's a safe answer to bathing in the tub. But remember: Never leave a child alone in the bathtub.

MEAL MESS HELPER

To avoid those messy spills under baby's high chair, put a plastic tablecloth under it at mealtime. Cleanup will be a breeze and you can even put the tablecloth in the washing machine with an old towel, detergent, and warm water. Hang to dry. This is a great tip when your toddler eats in Grandma's dining room!

Reaching over the table to cut up a little one's food can be awkward, so cut the job down to size by using a pizza cutter. It's much faster and easier!

CLEANING STUFFED ANIMALS

Dust heavily with baking soda or cornstarch and work in well with your fingers. Roll the toys in towels or place in a plastic bag and leave overnight. The next day use a clean brush to brush the toys thoroughly after removing from the bag. Doing this outdoors saves cleanup.

RATTLES AND TEETHERS

A great place to wash these is in the dishwasher. Tie them in the top basket and wash with the dishes.

FORMULA STAINS

On white clothes, apply undiluted lemon juice and lay the garment in the sun.

On colored clothes, make a paste of unseasoned meat tenderizer and cool water or an enzyme product from the laundry section at the grocery store. Apply and let sit for at least 30 minutes prior to laundering. Rubbing with a bar of wet Fels-Naptha® Laundry Bar Soap will also help.

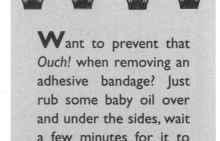

Want to prevent that *Ouch!* when removing an adhesive bandage? Just rub some baby oil over and under the sides, wait a few minutes for it to soak in, and presto! No more *Ouch!*

CLEANING TRAINING PANTS

To keep training pants white and odor-free, soak in a solution of 2 tablespoons of borax (available in the laundry section at the grocery store) and 1 gallon of hot water. Soak 1 hour prior to laundering.

TO REMOVE GUM OR SILLY PUTTY® FROM HAIR

Rub cold cream or petroleum jelly into the gum. Use a dry Turkish-towel-type rag to pull down on the hair strands and petroleum jelly. Work until all is out, then double shampoo.

That old reliable peanut butter also works great. Massage the gum and peanut butter together between your fingers until the gum is loosened and can be removed. Or freeze the area with ice cubes in a plastic bag, then pick out the gum.

CRAYON ON WALLS

Spray with WD-40® Lubricant. Wipe off with a paper towel. Wash with hot water and liquid dishwashing detergent, working in a circular motion. Rinse well.

CRAYON ON FABRIC

Place the stained surface down on a pad of paper towels and spray with WD-40®, let stand a few minutes, turn over, and spray the other side.

Again, let sit a few minutes. Apply dishwashing detergent and work into the stained area, replacing the toweling as it absorbs the stain. Wash in the hottest water for the fabric you are working with, using your regular laundry detergent and all-fabric bleach.

WATERCOLOR PAINT ON FABRIC

Brush and rinse as much of the watercolor from the surface as possible. Apply a soft-scrubbing product with a damp sponge and rub in a circular motion, working toward the center of the spot. Rinse and dry. If any stain remains, apply nail polish remover to a cotton ball, blot the stain, and rinse. Repeat as needed.

WATERCOLOR PAINT ON CARPET

Apply rubbing alcohol with a sponge, blotting the stained area lightly. Turn the sponge as the stain is absorbed. Repeat until no more stain is being removed. Most of the remaining stain can be removed with a damp sponge and soft-scrubbing product. Rinse carpet well.

MARKER MARKS ON APPLIANCES, WOOD, OR HARD PLASTIC

Wipe all stains with a damp sponge. If any stain remains, apply a soft-scrubbing product with a damp sponge, working in a circular motion, and rinse. If the stain remains, saturate a cotton ball with nail polish remover, blot the remaining stain, and rinse well. This works on paneling, painted wood, tile, and no-wax vinyl floors.

MARKER ON CARPET

Dampen a sponge with rubbing alcohol and use a blotting motion to absorb the marker, changing the sponge as needed. Apply a good carpet spotter, as directed on the can.

Remove red pop or juice stains on carpet or fabrics easily with Red Erase®. All-natural and safe for kids.

MARKER ON CLOTHING

Rinse the stain from the fabric with cold water until no more color is being removed. Place the fabric on paper towels and saturate with rubbing alcohol, using a cotton ball or small cloth to blot the stain. Replace the paper towels as often as needed to prevent restaining the fabric. Treat the stain with a lather from a bar of Fels-Naptha® Laundry Bar Soap and launder as usual.

CHALK ON HARD SURFACES

For colored or white chalk on masonry, painted surfaces, vinyl flooring, tile, plastic, and glass, brush and rinse as much of the chalk from the surface as possible. Remove the remaining stain with a damp sponge or cloth dipped in a soft-scrubbing product. Rinse surface well.

CHALK ON CARPET

Vacuum the area well, using the attachment hose to concentrate the suction over the chalk. If stain remains, use a good carpet-spotting product.

COLORED CHALK ON FABRIC

Place the stained area on a pad of paper towels and blot the spot with rubbing alcohol. Work in a lather of Fels-Naptha® Laundry Bar Soap and launder as usual.

GLUE ON CARPET AND FABRIC

For water-based glue such as Elmer's® School Glue, fold a paper towel to overlap the glue spot and satu-

Store baby clothes in empty diaper boxes. They have sizes printed on the outside, so no more guesswork!

rate to almost dripping with warm water. Place this on the glue spot and leave on for about 45 minutes to an hour to allow the glue to soften. Rub the glue spot with a wet rag in a circular motion to remove all the glue you can. Repeat this procedure until glue is removed. Follow with a good carpet spotter.

SILLY PUTTY® CLAY AND SIMILAR PRODUCTS ON CARPET AND FABRIC

Scrape off what you can with the dull edge of a knife. Spray with WD-40® Lubricant and let stand about 10–15 minutes. Scrape again. Respray as required, wiping up the stain with an old rag. Once you have removed the residue of the product, apply rubbing alcohol to the stain and blot, blot, blot. Reapply as necessary.

To remove from hard surfaces, spray with WD-40® Lubricant and wipe with a paper towel or old rag. Wipe any remaining stain with a cloth saturated with rubbing alcohol. Wash with a solution of dishwashing liquid and hot water, working in a circular motion. Rinse well.

WRITING ON PLASTIC TOYS AND DOLL FACES

Ink and marker are difficult to remove from plastic surfaces. Try applying a cotton ball saturated with rubbing alcohol. Let sit for 15 minutes and then rub. Sometimes using the pressure of a cotton swab dipped in alcohol helps. You can also try rubbing with a little cuticle remover on a soft cloth. Apply the cuticle remover, wait 10 minutes, then rub gently with the cloth.

Kid-related issues make up a large part of the questions that I receive. It has been proven to me many times that kids say and DO the darnedest things. A man called in during a radio show and said he had a problem he was hoping to solve before his wife got home so she wouldn't kill him. Visions of lipstick on his collar came to mind, but no, he had a problem that only a child could create.

While getting his son ready for bed, he realized that he had to go to the laundry room for pj's. He left his son and dirty diaper together in the crib while he ran to grab the pj's before putting on a fresh diaper. Now kids will color on anything and with anything, I can guarantee you. Since there were no crayons available, the boy, as boys will do, colored with what he had "on hand." I don't think his father appreciated the pictures, all in brown, on the wall, sides of the crib, and any fabric he could reach.

Thank goodness for father and son there is baking soda and lemon juice (it is nature's disinfectant) for washing down the wall and hard surfaces, Zout® Laundry Stain Remover to spray on the fabrics, and 20 Mule Team® Borax to add to the laundry to clean and disinfect.

Queen's advice: A child and his dirty diaper should be soon parted.

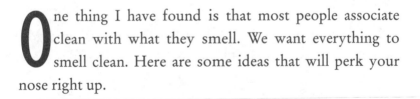

16

THE NOSE KNOWS—
ODOR CONTROL

O ne thing I have found is that most people associate clean with what they smell. We want everything to smell clean. Here are some ideas that will perk your nose right up.

PRODUCT CORNER

For those of you looking for a foolproof product to eliminate all odors, I highly recommend ODORZOUT®.

This is a 100 percent natural product that stops many

odors almost on contact—odors such as urine, mold, mildew, smoke, foot odor, skunk, paint, and virtually every other odor you can smell. It is made of blended natural zeolite minerals, contains no perfumes, and is 100 percent safe for use around children or pets. You can even use it in the cat litterbox. In my testing, I have found no odor it didn't work on. Call 800-88STINK for more information or ordering, or visit the website www.88stink.com. Also available at PETsMART nationwide.

BURNED FOOD

Boil a few slices of lemon in a saucepan to clear the air of the smell of burned food.

FRIED FOOD

This works on any fried-food odor, but the next time you fry fish, be sure to try it. Place a small bowl of white vine-

PALACE PENNYSAVERS

MAKE YOUR OWN AIR FRESHENER In a gallon jug, combine 1 cup baking soda, ¼ cup clear ammonia, and 1 tablespoon scent (use your imagination—any scented oils or extracts work). Slowly add 16 cups of warm water, label, and store. To use, pour well-shaken solution into a spray container and mist air as needed.

gar next to the stove when you fry foods. The odor seems to disappear.

REFRIGERATORS

To deodorize refrigerators, leave a bowl filled with clean clay cat litter or charcoal on the shelf to absorb odors. In refrigerators that are going to be shut off or moved, leave the door partially open at all times to allow air circulation, and put some litter or charcoal in an old nylon stocking and tie the top shut. Lay this in the refrigerator and it will control odors. For strong odors, nothing works better than dry, fresh coffee grounds. Put them in a bowl and leave in the refrigerator until odor disappears. This can be very effectively used in conjunction with the cat litter or charcoal.

CARS

If you smoke in the car, put a layer of baking soda in the bottom of the ashtray to absorb smoke odor. Empty it frequently. Dryer fabric-softener sheets placed under the seats also help to keep the smoke smell under control. For musty smells, put cat litter in a nylon stocking, tie the top shut, and place several under the seats or in the trunk.

WOOD TRUNKS, DRESSERS, AND CHESTS

Many times old wood trunks and dressers will have a musty mildew or old odor. To eliminate this, take a slice of white bread (yes, it has to be white), put it in a bowl, and cover with white vinegar. Leave enclosed in the trunk or drawers for twenty-four hours. If odor remains, repeat the process. If mildew odor persists in dresser drawers, shellac or varnish the inside of them and odor will be sealed in and eliminated.

HOME ODORS

Wintergreen oil is a wonderful deodorant. Purchase some at a health food store and put a few drops on cotton balls and stash in plants, decorative pieces, etc., around the house.

FAN-TASTIC

Ceiling fans are great at boosting the airflow of your air conditioner. They don't cost much unless you really want to be fancy, and with light maintenance they can last a long time.

Regular cleaning is important, especially if you run them all year long. Dust collects on the blades and the motor housing. A dustcloth or lamb's-wool duster, and the vacuum cleaner, will quickly remove the dirt. Turn the fan off before you attempt to clean it. Vacuum the blades and the housing thoroughly. Next, attack it with the cloth or duster to remove stubborn soil. If necessary, use a damp cloth or ACT Natural® Microfiber Cloth to wipe off the tacky dirt.

Many fans are self-oiling, but some require a squirt of lightweight lubricant on the motor shaft. Check out your owner's manual to see what you should do.

If the fan is wobbly or making noise, be sure that the screws are all tight after you clean it.

If you have a light fixture attached to the fan, be sure that the globe or globes are tightly attached to the fan. If dusting with the cloth or lamb's-wool duster doesn't clean them up, remove them and place on a towel in the sink and wash with mild detergent and water and dry thoroughly, carefully reattaching them to the fan when you are done.

AIR CLEANERS—DO THEY WORK?

I have had so many questions about air cleaners—are they worthwhile, do they work?

In this day and age of ozone warnings and dust particles in the air, I have become a fan of good air cleaners.

I particularly like to run them in the bedrooms and the nursery; your baby deserves clean air. Unfortunately, even though we don't like to talk about it, tons of dust, dust mites, and dry skin are lurking in our bedrooms. Dust and dust mites, in particular, can cause severe allergies in many people. If you are not sleeping well, if you are coughing, if your mate is snoring more, if you have a dry nose and throat, a good air cleaner may be the answer to your problems.

I have tried many different filters from the large, professional-type machines to the tall ones where you simply remove the metal catcher and wipe it off. The ones that you can readily buy with the removable metal dirt catcher are good for pet hair and larger dirt particles. Unfortunately, the dirt that causes the most trouble is the microscopic dust, pet dander, and dust mites. To actually clean the air of these things, you need a three-stage filter. This consists of a foam-type layer, to catch the larger things, that is washable and reusable. The second stage should be a true HEPA filter, not a HEPA-like or HEPA-type. To be sure you have a true HEPA filter, take the tip of your fingernail and press down on the white, pleated area of the HEPA filter. You should leave a small nail mark. On HEPA-like and HEPA-type filters, you will find a cardboard-type material and this will not indent and will not filter properly either. The third and last stage of the filter system should be a carbon filter, which will help to clean the odors in the air. An air cleaner with a curved shape will allow you to clean more air more efficiently.

Quality HEPA-filter air cleaners will come with a chart to indicate when the HEPA filter should be replaced. Since this air cleaner uses no chemicals, you can safely use it in the nursery—in fact, you should.

If your air cleaner comes with an ionizer, you should run that occasionally or not more than two hours a day. The ionizer will accumulate the dust and dirt into bigger pieces for capture, but with overuse can leave some of that dust and dirt hanging on your walls.

The important thing about any air cleaner that you purchase is to follow the directions that come with it and keep it clean. Once any air cleaner is clogged with dirt and dust, it can't do its job.

People are always asking me stinking questions. No, really! I get asked about odors and things that smell and stink all the time. One of my most unusual and, initially, perplexing questions came at a book signing in Orlando, Florida. Here's my stinking story.

A woman in the audience rose and approached the microphone. After waiting patiently for the people in front of her to finish, she stepped to the microphone, cleared her throat, and announced, "I have a moose head that stinks." Most of the audience gasped as we all pictured the head of a moose hanging on the wall in her home and, well, smelling. I asked her what kind of moose it was and she said she didn't know, it was just a moose head. I then asked if it was stuffed and she said no, not really, but every time Charlie put his head in it he could hardly stand the smell and neither could anyone around him. After more gasps from me and the audience, it turned out the moose head, now affectionately known as Prince, was part of a high school mascot costume. Unfortunately, Prince had been passed down for years from student to student without much thought to hygiene. If you picture years of kids stuffing themselves into a heavy, furry moose head in a hot and humid state like Florida, you can understand the problem. Prince was a moose that even the band steered clear of! Queen's solution . . . simple. Buy some ODORZOUT® and sprinkle inside of the moose head; wait 24 hours, vacuum it out, and reapply until the stench is gone. Then, after each wearing, sprinkle in ODORZOUT®, shake, and vacuum thoroughly before wearing it again. Odor is gone and ODORZOUT® is safe and nontoxic, no worries about chemicals. I hear that at the next game the band played "Hail to the Queen!"

17

HOT TIPS FOR IRONS AND IRONING BOARDS

CLEANING AN IRON THAT DOES NOT HAVE A NONSTICK SURFACE

Heat the iron to the hot, nonsteam setting. Run it over table salt sprinkled on a brown paper grocery bag.

You can also use nongel toothpaste. Apply it to a damp cloth and rub over the soleplate on a cool iron until starch buildup and ironing residue are removed. Rinse well.

For terrible buildup, burned-on fabric or starch, take the iron outside and cover all parts of the iron except sole-plate with paper. Spray oven cleaner directly onto the soleplate of a cool iron. Wait several minutes and then rinse off well with cool water and an old rag or sponge.

WITH A NONSTICK SURFACE

Use laundry pre-spotter. Rub on and rinse off well.

AFTER CLEANING

After cleaning your iron with any of these methods, re-member to rinse it well and then fill with water, heat on the heavy-steam setting, and iron over old fabric prior to using on clothes. This will remove any residue remaining in the vent holes.

CLEANING THE VENT HOLES

Many times the vent holes in the bottom of the iron will become clogged. Take a pipe cleaner and clean out each hole individually.

Always empty steam irons after each use to prevent clogging.

PALACE PENNYSAVERS

ENERGY-EFFICIENT IRONING Put aluminum foil under the ironing-board cover when you put it on the board. It will reflect heat onto the garments as you iron and cut ironing time.

CLEANING THE INTERNAL PARTS

Fill the steam iron with equal portions of water and white vinegar. Let it steam for several minutes. Disconnect the iron and let it sit for one hour. Empty and rinse with clear water using the same process. Be sure to iron over old fabric prior to ironing clothes.

KEEPING IRONING-BOARD COVERS CLEAN

To make covers last longer and stay clean longer, spray them with spray starch once the cover is on the board and iron the starch in well.

18

TAKING CHARGE OF ELECTRONIC EQUIPMENT

TELEPHONES

To clean and disinfect telephone receivers, apply Listerine® mouthwash with a soft cotton pad or rag. Do not rinse off. This is great advice for offices during cold and flu season.

TELEVISION SCREENS

Denatured alcohol (available at hardware stores) makes a great cleaner for many pieces of electronic equipment. To clean the TV screen, turn off the power to the TV. Apply alcohol to a rag or paper towel and wipe the screen thoroughly, then buff. Always follow any specific manufacturer's directions for cleaning the newer TV screens.

STOP DUST FROM SETTLING

Apply antistatic product to a rag and wipe the screen and cabinet, or mix 1 part liquid fabric softener to 4 parts water and apply with a soft cloth and buff.

RADIOS

These need to be dusted often. Clean them occasionally with denatured alcohol applied with a cotton ball. Do not use alcohol on wood.

CAMERAS

Cameras should always be stored in their cases when not in use. This prevents them from becoming dusty. Except for wiping off the outside of the lens with a cotton ball and a little alcohol, leave cleaning to the professionals.

VIDEOCASSETTE RECORDERS

These need to be kept free of dust to stay in good working order. It is best to cover them with a plastic cover when not in use. If the room is damp, keep silica packets (available from florists or many times found in new leather shoes or purses) on top of the VCR or DVD (keep these packets away from children). Clean occasionally using a cleaning tape to ensure good-quality pictures on playback. Store videotapes in cardboard or plastic cases to keep them clean and in good condition for playback or recording.

ANSWERING MACHINES

These need to be dusted with a lamb's-wool duster, particularly inside the machine. You can use an aerosol cleaner, but make sure that the machine is dry before you replace the cassette.

Never remove a working battery from a smoke detector, no matter how much you think you need it for something else. And do make sure to change your battery regularly— every 12 months is best. You can remind yourself to replace your battery each year by picking a significant date, such as a birthday, an anniversary, or even the first day of school.

FAX MACHINES

These also need to be kept dusted and occasionally wiped with denatured alcohol.

COMPACT DISCS

To keep your compact discs clean, mix 2 tablespoons of baking soda and 1 pint of water in a spray bottle. Shake well to mix and spray on the disc, wiping with a soft cloth. Do not wipe in a circular motion; wipe from the center hole in the disc out to the outside edge.

COMPUTERS

To avoid costly problems with computers, it is important that they be kept dust-free. Dust between the keys of your keyboard with a cotton swab, or vacuum with the duster brush on your vacuum or with a special computer vacuum that helps you get between the keys.

Mix 1 part water and 1 part alcohol and apply to the keys with a cotton swab. Don't overwet. Undiluted denatured alcohol may also be used in the same manner.

Dust the screen and spray with an antistatic product.

Make sure that computers are situated out of direct sunlight, which can cause overheating. Sunlight also makes it difficult for the user to see the computer screen clearly.

A SPECIAL REMINDER

Never clean any electronic equipment without unplugging it first!

19

ROGUES' GALLERY— THE CARE AND HANGING OF PICTURES

Pictures and paintings are part of the personal touches that make a house a home. Here are some ideas for hanging and cleaning pictures and oil and acrylic paintings.

FINDING THE STUD THE EASY WAY (NO, NOT *THAT* KIND OF STUD!)

When you are ready to hang a picture, especially a heavy one, it is a good idea to find a stud to hang it from. Take an

If you need to measure something but don't have a ruler or tape measure on hand, just pull out a dollar bill! Each bill is 6 inches long. You can take it from there!

electric razor and run it across the wall. You will notice a distinct difference in the sound of the razor going over hollow wall and the sound when it hits a stud. Use this whenever you need to find the stud to hang anything around the house.

KEEPING COCKEYED PICTURES STRAIGHT

Wind some adhesive tape around the center of the picture wire. The wire will be less likely to slip on the hanger.

Place masking tape on the back four corners of your picture and press against the wall. Wrap masking tape, sticky side out, around the middle of a round toothpick and place a few near the bottom, back side of the frame.

PREVENTING EXPERIMENTAL HOLES

Cut a paper pattern of each picture or mirror that you plan to hang and pin it to the wall. After you've found the correct positions for the hangers, perforate the paper with a sharp pencil to mark the wall.

When you want to avoid nail holes in the walls, hang

pictures with a sewing machine needle. They hold up to 30 pounds and leave almost no marks on the wall.

STAINING UNFINISHED PICTURE FRAMES

Stain them beautifully with ordinary liquid shoe polish. Apply one coat and let dry. Follow with another coat, then wax with a good paste wax. Brown shoe polish gives the wood a walnut glow, and oxblood emulates a mahogany or cherry color. Tan polish will look like a light maple. This hides scratches, too.

CLEANING GLASS-COVERED PICTURES

Never spray any cleaner directly on the glass; it may seep under and onto the picture. Spray a paper towel with window cleaner, wipe, and polish with a dry towel.

Polish glass with a used fabric-softener sheet to shine and deter dust.

CLEANING OIL AND ACRYLIC PAINTINGS

Give them an occasional dusting with a clean, lint-free cloth or a soft brush. Spot-clean if necessary with a barely damp rag or piece of white bread. If the painting is worth a lot of money or has sentimental value, take it to a professional. Even a soft dustcloth can snag and cause a chip.

GILT PICTURE FRAMES

Remove stains from gilt picture frames by rubbing gently with a cloth moistened in milk.

PHOTO EMERGENCY

If you have a picture that is stuck to the glass, immerse the glass and the photo in a pan of room-temperature water and keep testing until the photo pulls free. Don't try to rush it! Let the photo air-dry. Since most photo prints get a water bath during processing, there shouldn't be any damage, though this is not a 100 percent guarantee.

20
PAINT BY NUMBERS

One of the questions men ask me most frequently is how to get through the job of painting quickly and make it easier. Actually, there are things you can do to make the job go much more smoothly.

SHORT-TERM STORAGE

If you need to store a paintbrush or roller in the middle of a project or between coats of paint, place it in a tightly sealed plastic bag and place in the freezer. The brush or roller will not dry out for a day or two, and no cleanup is needed until you have completed the project.

PROTECT HARDWARE

When painting woodwork, cover doorknobs, locks, and other hardware with a generous coat of petroleum jelly. If the paint splashes where it shouldn't, it can easily be wiped up.

SPLATTER REMOVAL

For easy removal of paint splatters on windowpanes, use a round typewriter eraser with a brush on the end—it's safer than a razor and easy, too!

PAINTING SCREWS

To make painting screws from hardware easier, stick them in a piece of foam packing material. The screw heads will all be facing up, ready to be sprayed or painted in one coat.

CLEANING HANDS

Use vegetable oil to clean oil-based paints off hands. The oil is safer than paint thinner, has no fumes, and is mild to the skin. After using the oil, wash well with soap.

PREVENTING WHITE PAINT FROM YELLOWING

To stop white paint from yellowing with age, put several drops of black paint in for every quart of white paint. Mix well.

KEEP CANS CLEAN

Cover the rim of the paint can with masking tape if you are going to pour paint from the can. When you are done, remove the tape to clean the top.

DRIP REALIGNMENT

If you are painting from the can, punch two or three nail holes in the small groove in the top rim of your paint can. As you wipe the paint from your brush on the rim, the paint will drip back into the can instead of collecting in the groove and spilling over and down the sides of the can.

CLEAN BRUSHES IN A SECOND

To make a paintbrush easier to clean, wrap masking tape around the metal ferrule and about ½ inch over the bristles. Rather than drying on the bristles, paint will collect on the masking tape. To clean, remove the tape and clean the paint that remains on the brush.

GARBAGE GARMENT

Wear a garbage bag as a coverall when painting overhead. Cut a hole for head and arms. You can cover your head with an old shower cap. No more paint splatters on clothes and hair!

EASIER-OPENING CANS

When sealing the lid on a paint can, wipe a thin layer of petroleum jelly around the rim. This will allow the can to open easily the next time.

RECORD-KEEPING

Before you store leftover paint, list the rooms you have painted with it on the can. Touch-ups are easier if you don't

AN OUNCE OF PREVENTION

BRUSH UP A little bit of fabric softener will help prevent your paintbrushes from stiffening up. Clean up your brush after use, of course, then dip it into a solution of diluted fabric softener.

YIELD

have to try to figure out which can of paint you used for what.

PAINT-CATCHING WRISTBAND

If you paint like I do and have runs of paint going down your arms every time you paint over your head, wrap an old washcloth around your wrist, secure with a rubber band, and remove and throw away when you are done painting.

DRY BRUSHES COMPLETELY

If you soak your brush between painting sessions, be sure to drain out all of the liquid or you will have a dripping mess when you start painting again. One good way to do this is to stand the brush straight up in an empty can for a few minutes to let the fluid drip out or suspend it from a stick laid across the top of an empty can that is taller than the brush. To be absolutely sure that the brush is dry, take an old rag, wrap it around the brush, and squeeze the bristles from the top downward over the can.

WHERE TO START

Start painting at the top of the wall and work your way down. That way, if paint drips down, it can be smoothed out as you go.

WHEN TO START

No need to get up early to paint outside. You don't want to start painting until after the morning dew has evaporated. But remember, never paint in the direct sunlight.

21

THE GRILL DRILL

L et's talk about ways to make cooking on the grill easier and more fun.

PREVENT STICKING

Before you light the barbecue, spray the grill rack with nonstick cooking spray. This works great on gas or charcoal grills. Apply a liberal coat and food won't stick, making cooking and cleanup a lot easier.

CLEANING THE GRILL

To clean the grill surface when it is heavily caked with baked-on food, follow this procedure. Simply wrap the rack in a piece of heavy-duty aluminum foil, dull side facing out. Heat the barbecue to high heat and place the rack over the coals or flame for approximately 10 to 12 minutes. When you remove the foil after it has cooled, all the burned-on grease and food drippings will fall off and your rack will be spotless and ready to grill again.

IMMEDIATELY AFTER COOKING

Make a ball of aluminum foil and "scrub" the warm grill rack surface with it, taking care not to burn your fingers.

THE BATHTUB METHOD AND A LESS-MESSY VERSION

Many people recommend putting the grill rack in the bathtub filled with hot water, detergent, and ammonia. I find this a particularly messy way to do it because you have to clean the tub when you're done. If you do use this method, be sure to lay old rags or a garbage bag in the tub to prevent scratching the tub surface with the grill rack.

I suggest you try this method instead. Lay some paper towels moistened with undiluted ammonia on both sides of the rack. Put it in an appropriate-size plastic bag and seal. Leave it overnight, and the next day open the bag, away from your face—it stinks. Wipe down with the paper towels in the bag, wash with soapy water, and rinse.

Porcelain and coated grill racks can be cleaned by coating the rack with Zout® Stain Remover. Wait 30 minutes or so and then rub with a scrubbing sponge. Wash and rinse well.

KEEPING PAN BOTTOMS CLEAN

Before setting a pan on the grill rack to warm barbecue sauce or cook additional foods, rub the pan bottom with bar soap and it will be easier to clean the soot off when you are done.

Pine, spruce, or other evergreen wood should never be used for barbecuing. These woods, when burning or smoking, can add harmful tar and resins to the food. Only hardwoods should be used for smoking and grilling, such as oak, pecan, hickory, maple, cherry, alder, apple, or mesquite, depending on the type of meat being cooked.

CLEANING PERMANENT BRIQUETTES

Flip the briquettes occasionally and ignite the grill with the cover closed. Allow it to burn at a high setting for about 15 minutes.

GREASE SPLATTERS

For cement or wood patios, keep a container of salt nearby when barbecuing. Should grease spatter or drip, immediately cover with salt. Sweep up and reapply until grease is absorbed. Scrub with dishwashing liquid and rinse.

KEEPING THE OUTSIDE OF THE GRILL CLEAN

This is such a fast, easy way to clean the outside of the grill. It works well on charcoal and gas grills and will make them look almost like new. Take some GOJO® Crème Waterless Hand Cleaner (available at grocery stores, hardware stores, and home centers) and rub it on the outside of a cool grill with an old rag or paper towel. Work it into the metal well, paying special attention to any grease or barbecue sauce spots. Do not rinse; instead, take paper towels and buff the grill surface and watch as the dirt is replaced by a great shine.

KEEPING THE GLASS GRILL WINDOW CLEAN

Many gas grills have glass windows in them. Of course, once you use the grill a few times, you can no longer see through the window! To clean this, spray the inside of the glass with oven cleaner. Wait a few minutes and then scrub and rinse well. On the outside of the glass use GOJO® Crème Waterless Hand Cleaner and buff well.

22

EVERYTHING UNDER THE SUN FOR PATIO FURNITURE

No matter what part of the country you live in, at some time you have to clean the outdoor furniture. Follow this advice to make the job go faster.

FURNITURE CUSHIONS

There are several ways to clean outdoor furniture cushions. In a spray bottle combine 1 teaspoon of dishwashing liquid and 1 teaspoon of borax per quart of warm water. Spray this on the cushion on both sides and let it sit for about 15 minutes. Then take out the hose and, using a strong spray, rinse the solution and the dirt off the cushions. Put them back on the chairs and set them out of the direct sun to dry. Once they have dried to just damp, apply a good coating of Scotchgard® Fabric Protector™ (available at grocery stores and home centers) to protect the cushions and make cleaning easier the next time. Vacuum the cushions as needed to remove dust between cleanings.

You can also test your favorite carpet spotter in a small area. If it does not cause any damage, clean according to package directions.

ALUMINUM

Although it doesn't rust, aluminum can become dull and pitted when left outdoors. To clean and restore the shine, scrub the frames with a plastic scrubber soaked in detergent or a soap-filled steel wool pad, then rinse and dry.

ALUMINUM WITH BAKED-ENAMEL FINISH

Use a sponge soaked in detergent and wash well, rinse, and dry. To protect, apply a coat of good-quality car wax. This will make cleaning easier and maintain the

shine. It can be used on tables with a baked-enamel finish, too.

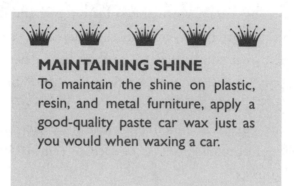

MAINTAINING SHINE
To maintain the shine on plastic,
resin, and metal furniture, apply a
good-quality paste car wax just as
you would when waxing a car.

CANVAS

Soiled canvas seats and chair backs are usually machine washable, but be sure to put them back on the furniture when they
are still damp to maintain their shape. To clean canvas that
you cannot put in the washing machine, such as large seats,
backs, or awnings, run a scrub brush back and forth across a
bar of Fels-Naptha® Laundry Bar Soap. Rub this back and
forth across the canvas and then rinse well. This will even remove bird droppings and, many times, the staining, too.

PLASTIC

Wash with a good all-purpose cleaner and water, then rinse
with water and dry. An alternative for white furniture is

automatic-dishwasher detergent and warm water (1 gallon warm water to 3 tablespoons automatic-dishwasher detergent). Wash and let solution sit on the furniture for 15 minutes or so, then rinse and dry.

23

ALL HANDS ON DECKS

Acertain amount of routine maintenance is required to keep your backyard deck structurally sound, safe, and looking its best.

Though other types of lumber may have been used, chances are that your deck is built of cedar, redwood, or pressure-treated yellow pine. These are the most commonly used materials for decks because they are resistant to rot and insect damage. When exposed to the elements for extended periods, any wood will show signs of weathering. Even if the deck was originally treated with stain or a preservative, this treatment eventually needs to be renewed.

INSPECT AND PROTECT

The first thing you need to do once the weather turns nice is to inspect the deck surfaces for any splintering, which you will need to sand. Pay special attention to the railing.

You'll find many stains and sealers designed for decks. Several manufacturers now offer products called deck brighteners, which actually bleach the surface to remove stains and weathering on wood surfaces. Apply these products carefully, following the instructions. Usually you will brush the product on with a stiff bristle brush and rinse off thoroughly prior to applying any finish coating.

Sealers protect the deck from moisture and are available in clear or tinted varieties to act as a stain. Sealers require periodic renewal to maintain protection.

Now go over the actual decking to be sure it is tight and in place, fixing whatever is required. Finally, if no repair or staining is needed, follow some of these suggestions to give the deck a good cleaning.

If leaves and other debris are on the deck, either sweep or use a blower to remove them.

HOSE OFF THE DECK

With a garden hose and a strong—and preferably long-handled—brush, use the strongest spray setting on the nozzle to break up dirt on the surface. Follow this with the brush to loosen any stubborn soil. This works especially well with two people, who can take turns hosing and scrubbing.

KILL MILDEW

Check the condition of the wood. Green or black areas indicate mold and mildew. To remove mold and mildew from the wood, you will need either a commercial deck-cleaning product (which may be purchased at your local home center) or you can prepare your own using a mixture of 1 cup trisodium phosphate (available at janitorial supply stores and home centers), 1 gallon of oxygen-type bleach (safer to use than chlorine bleach), and 1 gallon of hot water. The bleach will kill the mildew and the TSP will thoroughly clean the wood surface. You can apply this with a garden sprayer or mop it on.

First wet down the deck with the hose and then apply the cleaning solution. Spread the solution evenly and scrub with the brush you used earlier. Let the solution sit for about 15 minutes and then hose off. Repeat the wetting, bleaching, and rinsing as necessary until the entire deck is clean. Make sure you do stairs, handrails, and any other deck parts.

After you have done the entire deck, I recommend that you hose down the grass and any plants surrounding it to remove any solution that has dripped on them. No damage should be done to plants, but rinsing is a good precaution.

If you have used a garden sprayer, be sure to wash it out well and rinse the brush before storing.

QUICK CLEANING

To give the deck a quick cleaning during the use season, mix up a gallon of hot water and ¼ cup of any good-quality household cleaner, or 1 gallon of hot water, 1 tablespoon of dishwashing liquid, and ¼ cup of borax. Mop the deck down with one of these solutions and rinse well. Again, be sure to rinse plants and grass down.

REMOVING SAP FROM AN UNFINISHED WOOD DECK

Tree sap can be a problem on wood decks. To remove it, apply mineral spirits with an old rag, rub, and wash off with dishwashing liquid and water (1 teaspoon of dishwashing liquid to 1 quart of hot water). Rinse well.

24

CONCRETE SOLUTIONS FOR CLEANING CEMENT DRIVEWAYS AND PATIOS

One question everyone asks is how to clean cement driveways, garage floors, and patios. The best time to clean cement is when the temperature is between 50 and 75 degrees and the direct sun is not shining on it. Take this into consideration when using the cleaning methods in this chapter.

GRAB THE DUST ON CEMENT

To make quick work of sweeping a cement garage floor or patio, pick up some sweeping compound at either a janitorial supply store, hardware store, or home center. The sweeping compound will "grab" the dust instead of your spreading it in the air as you sweep. When you're done, just sweep it into a dustpan and throw out.

KITTY LITTER™—
A GARAGE FLOOR'S BEST FRIEND

Cat box litter, either regular clay or clumping, is wonderful for absorbing liquid spills, especially oil of any kind. Simply pour it on the spot and then—the secret to success—grind it into the spot with your foot. Do this for several weeks whenever you think of it. Allow it to absorb all of the oil that it can. Then sweep up. Repeat the process if necessary.

OLD STAINS ON CEMENT

Apply a spray-and-wash product and leave it on for 5–10 minutes. Sprinkle with laundry detergent, scrub with a stiff brush or broom, then rinse.

Another good method is to make a paste of hot water

and automatic-dishwasher detergent. Scrub it into the spot and let it soak for at least one hour or overnight. Add additional water and scrub, then rinse well.

REMOVING THE TOUGHEST STAINS

Use oven cleaner to remove the toughest spots. Spray it on, keeping your face well back. Let it stand for 15 minutes and then scrub with a stiff brush or broom and hose off. Repeat if necessary. Do not allow children or pets in the area when using this method. Rinse cement and brush with plenty of water. Do not combine other cleaning products with the oven cleaner until it is rinsed well with water.

REMOVING RUST FROM CONCRETE

Wet the concrete and sprinkle with lemon Kool-Aid®. Cover with plastic and soak for 15 minutes. Remove plastic, scrub with a brush, and rinse well.

Another method that may work for you is applying ZUD® Heavy Duty Cleanser. This can be purchased at the store in the cleanser section. Make a paste with warm water and work in well with a brush. Let soak for 30 minutes and then scrub with additional hot water and rinse well.

If the rust stain is really bad, you will have to use a solution of 10 parts water to 1 part muriatic acid. Let this sit 2–3 hours and then scrub with a stiff, nonmetallic brush. Use extreme caution if you use this method. Wear goggles, gloves, and old clothes, and rinse, rinse, rinse! Keep children and pets away from the area while using the acid.

25

AT THE CAR WASH

AUTO QUICK TIPS

Stain Guard

Before long trips, spray the front of your car, where the bugs collect, with nonstick cooking spray. This will stop bugs from sticking, and bugs and dirt can easily be washed off.

Cleaning the Windshield

Clean your windshield with baking soda and water prior to washing the car. White vinegar added to a wet, lint-free rag will remove grease film and give you a streak-free shine.

Bug Scraper

Save the plastic net bags from produce such as onions to scrub the window when it is spattered with bugs. Keep a couple in the car to use at the gas station when washing your windows and then throw them away. Great to have on hand when you're traveling.

Removing Tar

Saturate tar spots with linseed oil. Let soak and then rub with an old rag or paper towel moistened with the oil.

Removing Bumper Stickers

Use a blow-dryer to heat the sticker, then use a flat edge, such as an old credit card, and start peeling. Continue to heat and peel. Remove residue with nail polish remover.

Chrome

If you have dirty chrome on your car, simply dampen a piece of aluminum foil and rub. This is a great way to remove rust, too.

Battery Corrosion Stopper

Scrub the battery terminals and the holder with ½ cup baking soda combined with 2 cups warm water. When dry, apply petroleum jelly to the area.

Preventing Doors from Freezing

Spray the rubber gaskets around the door and trunk with nonstick cooking spray. This will keep water out and also keep the gaskets supple. Remember this trick if you plan on having the car washed in cold weather.

Making Windshield-Washer Solvent

This can be used in the windshield-washer container in your car—winter or summer. It will not freeze and is a great cleaner. Combine 1 quart rubbing alcohol, 1 cup water, and 2 tablespoons of liquid dishwashing detergent or laundry detergent. This should not freeze even at 30 degrees below zero.

Removing Salt Residue from Carpet

Combine a 50/50 solution of white vinegar and water. Apply to carpet and blot. Reapply as necessary.

General Interior Cleaning

Test your favorite carpet spotter according to package directions.

For Leather Upholstery

Wet a soft cloth with warm water and rub it across a wet bar of Dove® moisturizing soap several times. Wash the seats thoroughly, rinsing out the cloth and reapplying the soap as it becomes soiled. Do not rinse; instead, dry with a soft cloth.

You can also use a fantastic leather cleaner called Leather CPR™ Cleaner and Conditioner. It can be used on any color leather and will breathe life into aged car upholstery as it cleans and helps prevent cracking.

Quick Waxing

You don't want to spend more time waxing your car than necessary, so try this trick. Before waxing, park the car in the sun to warm (it shouldn't be too hot to touch), then move it into the shade when you are ready to wax it. The warm surface will make the wax go on smooth and fast.

PROFESSIONAL INTERIOR CLEANING

To really give your car a complete cleaning, rent an extraction machine at the hardware store or home center and clean upholstered seats and carpet thoroughly. Be sure to leave the windows down to allow the interior to dry completely.

26

DO AWAY WITH WINDOW PAINS

To achieve professional results you need to use the same tools the professionals use. You can find all of these things at either a janitorial supply store (look in the yellow pages) or a hardware store.

USE THE RIGHT TOOLS

Squeegee

A good squeegee is an absolute must. Don't be fooled into thinking that a cheap plastic squeegee or a car windshield squeegee will do the job—they won't! The best size to start with is a 12- or 14-inch squeegee. This will work well on most windows, and once you have mastered this size, you can move up to an 18-inch for large-paned windows and down to a 6-inch for small French panes.

Scrubber

A good scrubber is a plus. This tool looks like a squeegee wearing a fluffy coat. It is used to wet and clean the window prior to using the squeegee. If you do not want to invest in this, be sure you buy a good natural sponge.

Rag or Chamois

Use a dry rag or chamois for drying the squeegee rubber (blade) and the edges of the glass.

Scraper

Use a window scraper for removing paint, concrete, and other stubborn debris. If you don't purchase this, you can use a good medium- to fine-grade steel-wool pad. If you use one, be sure the pad and the window are soapy wet. Never use one of those

BAD NEWS
Remember, no matter what you have heard about cleaning windows with newspaper, don't do it. It is dirty and messy, leaving newsprint all over white window trim and paint.

scrub pads that you use on dishes; this will scratch the glass. Never use steel wool on tinted glass.

Extension Pole

If you have difficult, high, hard-to-reach windows, you might consider an extension pole made for a squeegee. This will enable you to stand on the ground and reach the high windows without a ladder.

Bucket and TSP

Fill a bucket with water and add TSP (trisodium phosphate) or dishwashing detergent (2 or 3 squirts).

LET'S GET STARTED

Fill your bucket with warm water and add the TSP or dishwashing liquid.

Be sure you have all the necessary equipment laid out and ready for use.

Follow the steps listed below, in order. You'll be cleaning like a pro in no time!

Dip your scrubber or sponge into the cleaning solution and wash the window thoroughly, using a very wet steel-wool pad to remove any stubborn spots, such as bug stains. You do not have to press too hard on the steel-wool pad. Rewet the window so you will have time to squeegee the window before it dries. Try not to clean in the direct sunlight, as it will cause streaking and spotting.

Tilt the squeegee at an angle so that 2 inches of rubber blade touches the glass. Start at the top corner and draw the squeegee along the top edge of the window.

Wipe the squeegee blade on a sponge, start on the dry surface close to the frame, and draw the squeegee down to within about 3 inches of the bottom of the glass.

Repeat this stroke until you have squeegeed all of the glass. Be sure you overlap each stroke and wipe the squeegee blade after each stroke.

Soak up excess water with a well-rinsed sponge.

Do the same thing you did at the top of the glass, this time working at the bottom of the glass.

Have your rag or chamois handy to wipe the window edges if needed. If you see a streak on the window, let it dry, then use a poly/cotton rag, such as an old T-shirt, to polish it out.

SPRAY-AND-WIPE CLEANING SOLUTIONS

If you prefer to wash your windows the spray-and-wipe way, here are a couple of good cleaning solutions.

Polishing Glass or Removing Screen and Bug Stains

- Make a thin paste of baking soda and water, rub onto the glass, rinse well, and dry with a soft cloth.

• Use some Lava® Soap on a damp soft cloth, rinse, and dry.

Easy Window Cleaner

Combine:

    2 quarts warm water

    ½ cup cornstarch

Apply to window with a sponge and buff dry with paper towels or soft, lint-free rags.

Tough-Job Window Cleaner

Combine:

    1 pint rubbing alcohol

    2 tablespoons clear ammonia

    2 tablespoons dishwashing liquid

Apply to the window using a nylon-covered sponge, rinse, and buff dry. Great for hard-water spots.

QUICK TIP

Use a dry blackboard eraser on a dry window or mirror after cleaning to banish any streaks you've left behind!

SCREEN SAVERS

Most people hose screens down to clean them. This just moves the dirt from one part of the screen to another. Here's a better way. Just soap the screen with a sponge dipped in a pail of warm water containing 2 tablespoons of dishwashing liquid, ¼ cup of ammonia, and 2 tablespoons of borax. Really suds up the screen. Now lay a rag on the ground and gently tap the screen on it. Most of the soapy water containing the dirt will come off this way. To finish, rinse the screen with the hose and stand to dry, or rag dry.

27

FLOWER POWER

MAKING FRESH FLOWERS LAST LONGER

To make fresh flowers from your garden or floral arrange-
ments from the florist last longer, use the following recipe.
Remove any foliage below the waterline, trim the stem ends
periodically, and keep the solution fresh, and your flowers
will live longer.

Combine:

    1 quart of water
    2 tablespoons of lemon juice
    1 tablespoon sugar
    ½ teaspoon liquid bleach

Add the solution to the flower container and enjoy. If you have an arrangement from the florist, add this solution each time you add water.

If you don't have the above ingredients on hand, add 2 ounces of Listerine® mouthwash per gallon of water.

To make cut flowers last longer without shedding, spray with hair spray. Hold the spray can about a foot away from the flowers and spray in an upward direction to prevent the flowers from drooping.

CLEANING VASES

To easily clean a flower vase, fill with warm water and add one or two denture-cleaning tablets, depending on the size of the vase. Let it soak at least an hour or overnight. Wash, rinse, and dry well. If you don't have any denture-cleaning tablets, throw in a handful of dry rice and some white vinegar and shake, shake, shake. Let soak with vinegar and warm water if necessary. Wash and rinse the vase well.

TRANSPORTING FRESH FLOWERS

If you are taking fresh flowers from your garden as a gift, or to the office, fill a balloon with water, put the stems in, and secure the neck of the balloon to the stems with a rubber band, twist tie, or ribbon. Poking the stems through a paper doily will also hold the stems in place and make an attractive presentation. Your flowers will arrive fresh-looking at their destination with no spilled water to worry about!

THE DIRT ON FLOWERPOTS

When planting flowers in a pot with a drainage hole in the bottom, line the bottom of the pot with enough coffee filters to cover it. Add a few pebbles and then add the soil. When you water the plant, the dirt won't run out the bottom.

FLOWER FILLER

When planting shallow-rooted flowers in a large pot, line the bottom with coffee filters and pebbles, fill the pot ⅓ full of packing peanuts, then fill with soil. The pot will be much lighter to move and you won't require as much soil to fill the pot.

LET THEM SHINE
To shine indoor-plant leaves, wipe gently with glycerin. Another great way to add shine is to wipe leaves with a mixture of half milk and half water. Do not use oil on plant leaves, as it attracts dust and dirt.

HEALTHFUL WATER

When you boil eggs, save the water to water your plants. It is full of minerals.

Cold coffee or tea combined with water provides an acidic drink for your plants. (Be sure it doesn't run out on the carpet.)

Water from an aquarium provides excellent fertilizer for plants.

Club soda that has lost its fizz is good for plants.

Going on vacation? Stand plants in the sink or bathtub, depending on the number you have. Be sure they are in pots with a hole in the bottom. Add a few inches of water to the tub and plants will automatically be watered while you are gone. To preserve the tub finish, lay an old towel in the bottom to set plants on.

UNBUGGED

If bugs are a problem on indoor plants, spray the soil with insect spray and immediately cover the plant with a plastic bag. Leave in place for a couple of days and then uncover.

WINDOW BOXES AND PATIO FLOWERPOTS

These are easy to keep clean. After you plant the flowers in the pots, put a layer of gravel or marbles on top. When you water or it rains, the dirt won't splash all over the plants, pots, patio, or porch.

HANGING PLANTS

To water hanging plants with ease and without the mess of water running all over, use ice cubes. The cubes melt slowly and won't allow water to run out onto the floor or patio.

WEED PREVENTION

To kill weeds growing in sidewalk cracks, pour boiling salt water on them. Use a mixture of ¼ cup salt to 2 quarts water.

To prevent the weeds from growing in the cracks, sprinkle salt into the cracks.

CLEANING ARTIFICIAL FLOWERS

To really clean and remove soil from artificial flowers, dried silk or polyester, place them in a bag with table salt. Add salt in proportion to the size of the flowers. Close the bag and shake the flowers in the salt for several minutes, or longer if the flowers are heavily soiled. Shake gently to remove the salt. The salt won't look dirty when you are done, but if you run water into it, you will be surprised how much dirt has been removed from the flowers.

You can also place silk flowers in a pillowcase, tie a knot in it, and put it in the clothes dryer on "air fluff" or "air only" for about 15–20 minutes.

Spray polyester flowers with acrylic spray from the craft store and they will resist soiling. If they get very dusty, wash under a mild stream of running water, shake, and stand up to dry.

For large fabric trees and plants, I have had success misting (no harsh spray) with the hose. Let dry well and bring back into the house.

28

BUG OUT—
USER-FRIENDLY
PEST CONTROL

Are the bugs bugging you? Are the pests pestering you? You can control bugs without chemicals the safe, environmentally friendly way. When planting flowers or controlling insects inside the house, keep this guide handy.

INSECT REPELLENT

When using insect sprays, especially those containing deet, try spraying clothes instead of skin—it's much safer, especially for children.

OR TRY VINEGAR

A wonderful substitute for insect repellent is white vinegar. Apply it liberally to the skin with a cotton ball. Bugs hate the way you taste and the smell of the vinegar disappears once it dries. Great for kids!

To trap and drown snails and slugs, place a shallow dish of beer slightly below grade so that the lip of the dish is even with the soil. The pests will go for a drunken swim and never emerge, but they will die happy.

ANTS

For ants on the counter, wipe the counter down with undiluted white vinegar.

To prevent ants from coming in the house or getting into cupboards, sprinkle dried mint or red pepper where they are entering the house and in the cupboards.

To get rid of anthills, pour 3 gallons of boiling water down them. This is best done when the ants are active and near the surface. Do not do this close to flowers or they will die, too.

Another way to kill ants is to mix a combination of 50 percent borax and 50 percent confectioners' sugar. Place this on cardboard or a piece of board near the anthill. The ants are attracted by the sugar and carry the fatal borax/sugar combination back to the nest to feed the queen and other ants. Soon all are dead. A note of caution: Do not place this where children or pets may ingest this mixture. Borax is found in the laundry aisle at the grocery store as a laundry additive, not as a pesticide.

When ants find food, they lay down a chemical trail, called a pheromone, so that other ants can find their way from the nest to the food source. Worker ants may live 7 years, and the queen (long live the queen!) may live as long as 15 years.

APHIDS

Mix nonfat dry milk with water according to the directions on the box, then put in a spray bottle and apply it to the leaves of your plants. As the milk dries, the aphids get stuck in the milky residue and die. You can rinse the plants from time to time with the hose. This will not harm your plants and offers an inexpensive solution to a big problem.

APHIDS AND SPIDERS

Wash off the plant with a mild solution of dishwashing liquid and water. Try a ratio of ½ teaspoon dishwashing liquid to 1 quart water. Flush leaves, including undersides, with the solution. Do not rinse off.

APHIDS AND WHITEFLIES

These bugs are attracted to bright yellow and can be trapped by placing a yellow board or other yellow objects such as yellow poster board, oleo lids, or sticks painted yellow, coated with

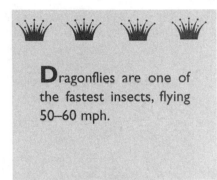

Dragonflies are one of the fastest insects, flying 50–60 mph.

heavy motor oil, petroleum jelly, or Tack-Trap® near susceptible plants. Recoat when the traps dry out.

APHIDS ON ROSES

Use 1½ teaspoons of baking soda per pint of water and apply every seven days. This method is user-, earth-, and child-friendly.

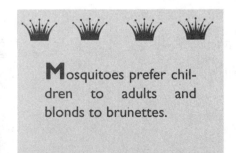

Mosquitoes prefer children to adults and blonds to brunettes.

COCKROACHES

To keep cockroaches out of the cupboards, place some bay leaves on the shelves.

Kill cockroaches with a mixture of ⅓ borax, ⅓ cornmeal, ⅓ flour, and a dash of powdered sugar. Sprinkle

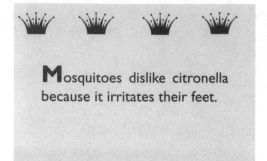

Mosquitoes dislike citronella because it irritates their feet.

this in crevices under sinks and vanities where cockroaches love to hide. Remember, keep this away from children and animals.

You can also try this formula for cockroaches: Mix powdered boric acid with sugar and powdered nondairy creamer. I use a mixture of 50 percent boric acid to 25 percent each sugar and creamer. This is inexpensive and relatively safe, but it should be kept away from children and pets. Sprinkle the mixture in all the dark, warm places that cockroaches love—under sinks and stoves, behind refrigerators, in cabinets and closets, and so on. The roaches will walk through the powder and then clean themselves, much the way a cat preens. Once they ingest the powder they die.

GRASSHOPPERS

To deter grasshoppers, plant basil around the flower bed borders. Grasshoppers will eat the basil and leave the plants alone.

National Poison Control Center: 1-800-222-1222
This emergency line connects anyone in the United
States, 24 hours a day, 7 days a week, to the closest
regional Poison Control Center.

SAFETY FIRST

If you are using commercial pest control products, look for
those containing the green cross or the words *safe for people, pets, and food surfaces.*

Dispose of pesticide containers safely:

- Follow directions printed on the package.
- For containers with screw-on lids, rinse out well
  (outside), then puncture the container to prevent
  reuse.
- Wrap the container in several plastic bags, seal,
  then dispose of the container in the garbage can.

29

YOUR BEST FOOT FORWARD

What article of clothing gets more wear and tear than our shoes? Many of us have a favorite pair of tennis shoes that we live in. When we come home, we take them off after a hot day at work, and our family leaves the room making comments about a skunk smelling better. Now, there is a quick, easy answer to shoe odor. Taking good care of shoes will make them look better, of course, but it will also extend the life of the shoes.

CLEANING AND DEODORIZING SHOES

This method will work with any shoe. First, sprinkle some baking soda in the shoe, then place it in a plastic bag and freeze it for a night or two. Allow the shoe to come to room temperature (unless you want to cool your feet), then shake out the baking soda and wear. It is a good idea to leave the baking soda in the shoe until the next wearing.

STRETCHING SHOES

Here's another freezer tip for the pair of shoes that pinches your toes. For each shoe use a heavy-duty zip-closure bag, or double up two of them and put them in each shoe. Carefully pour water into the bags, until the toe area is full. Close the bags securely so the water doesn't seep out and get the shoes wet. To help prevent the outside of the shoes from getting wet, put each shoe in a plastic bag. Place the shoes in the freezer for at least 24 hours. As the water freezes, it expands, and as it does this, the shoes will expand

PALACE PENNYSAVERS

IF PLASTIC TIPS FALL OFF YOUR SHOELACES Easy—twist the ends of the shoelaces and dip in clear nail polish.

and stretch. To remove the bags of water, you will need to allow the shoes to defrost.

CLEANING WHITE CANVAS SHOES

Apply a paste of automatic-dishwasher detergent mixed with hot water to the shoes. Allow to soak at least 30 minutes, then scrub surface with a nail brush or toothbrush. Rinse well and allow to dry. Dry the shoes out of the direct sun. You can also put the shoes in the washing machine with several old white towels and launder as usual after soaking and brushing. To keep the shoes clean, set them on paper and apply several coats of spray starch or fabric protector. They will stay clean longer and soil will wash out more easily.

CLEANING WHITE LEATHER ATHLETIC SHOES

These can be cleaned easily with whitewall-tire cleaner. Take the shoes outside if possible or spray over newspaper.

No need to buy costly potions to cure a mild case of athlete's foot. Just clean feet daily and sprinkle them— and your socks!—with some cornstarch. Worked well for Grandma and Grandpa!

Let sit 2–3 minutes, then wipe with paper towels or old rags. Remember, whitewall-tire cleaner is a bleaching product, so rinse shoes thoroughly before wearing in the house on carpet. Pay special attention to the soles.

POLISHING WHITE LEATHER

Before polishing, clean well. To remove scuffs, try an art gum eraser or a paste of baking soda and water. To cover scuffs that won't come off, use liquid typewriter correction fluid prior to polishing. Prep the shoes for white polish by rubbing them with the cut side of a raw potato. The potato will help the polish go on smoothly and cover scuff marks.

WHEN YOU'RE OUT OF SHOE POLISH

Reach for the furniture polish. Take a rag and spray liberally with furniture polish. Rub the shoe well and buff. In a real hurry, use baby wipes! Rub on and buff.

FIXING SCUFFS AND TEARS ON SHOES

If there's a black mark on your shoe, try a dab of nail polish remover, rubbing alcohol, or lighter fluid on a clean cloth. For areas where the color is removed, try using a marker in the same color. Wipe immediately after applying with a paper towel and then polish.

SCUFFS ON GOLD OR SILVER SHOES

Use an old, dry toothbrush with white toothpaste to remove the scuff; polish with clear polish or furniture polish.

POLISHING PATENT LEATHER

Rub petroleum jelly into patent leather and buff with a soft cloth. It not only polishes, it prevents cracking.

SCUFF MARKS ON VINYL OR PLASTIC SHOES

Use lighter fluid. Be sure to dispose outside the rag or paper towel you use.

TO KEEP CHILDREN'S SHOES TIED

Dampen the laces with a spray of water before you tie them. This allows you to tie the bows tighter and the laces will stay in place.

30

TURNING DOWN THE HEAT ON FIRE DAMAGE

I honestly hope that you never have any reason to do anything more than just glance through this chapter, but if you ever have a fire in your home, remember it's here. I spent 15 years as the owner of a disaster restoration company in Michigan, and I can tell you that in those first hours after a fire it's all you can do to remember your name.

The fire truck has just left and there you stand amid what once was your home and is now a smelly, wet, black mess that you hardly recognize. You want to sit down and have a good cry, but there isn't anyplace clean to sit. What do you do now? Is everything ruined? This chapter will help you deal with the emotional turmoil and give you sound information about what you, as the homeowner, need to do.

JUST IN CASE

First, as soon as you are done reading this, put your home-owner's policy, along with your agent's name and phone number, in a fireproof box or bank safe-deposit box. This enables you to easily find them and protects them from being destroyed in the fire. Make notes from this chapter and put them with your insurance information.

GET ON THE PHONE

After the fire is out, call your insurance agent or the 800 number that is often provided on your policy to report claims.

Call immediately. It may seem like the damage couldn't be worse, but it could. After a fire there can be ongoing damage from acid soot residue. Fire produces two main pollutants—nitrous oxide (from burning wood, food, etc.) and sulfur dioxide (from burning plastics and petroleum by-products, etc.). When these pollutants combine with moisture and humidity, they form acid! Within hours this can cause substantial and continuing damage. Prompt attention from your local disaster restoration firm will eliminate the problem and prevent further damage to valuables. Disaster restoration companies are listed in your phone directory and are available 24 hours a day for emergencies. They will preserve, protect, and secure surfaces that may be subject to continuing damage and will work with your insurance adjuster to estimate the damage.

WHAT IS AN INSURANCE ADJUSTER?

The insurance adjuster works for the insurance company. He is an expert in smoke damage, such as chimney fires, furnace backups, and actual fire damage. He will help you decide what can be saved and what can't. He will require a written estimate from a disaster restoration company and any contractors or dry cleaners who will participate in the cleanup. Sometimes more than one estimate will be requested.

During this time you will be receiving all kinds of comments and advice from friends, relatives, and even strangers. Ignore it! Your insurance adjuster is a professional and knows the best way to handle smoke damage. The adjuster may even be able to give you advice on a company that they have dealt with before if you are unsure of whom to call.

DISASTER RESTORATION COMPANIES

Disaster restoration companies (i.e., cleaning companies) do two types of cleaning: structural and contents cleaning. Structural cleaning is wall-washing, carpet cleaning, cupboards—the things you can't remove from the house when you move. Contents cleaning is the upholstery, hard furniture, dishes, clothes, etc.—things you take with you when you move. The company will provide a complete estimate to the insurance company and a copy to you.

Once coverage is confirmed and appropriate authorizations are secured, the cleaning and repairs will take place as quickly as possible. This will include dry cleaning, laundry, and deodorization, also covered in this chapter.

PAYMENT

After completion of all the cleaning and restoration, the insurance company will generally issue a check in your name and in the name of the firm that did the work. Once the work is satisfactory, you sign over the checks.

DEODORIZATION

Deodorization is one of the most important parts of any smoke damage cleanup. Everything smells—even your clothes.

First, the initial odor must be brought under control immediately to make the house habitable, if you are able to live in it during the restoration.

During any reconstruction, exposed interior wall sections will be deodorized and any singed wood will be sealed to prevent odor. In serious fires, deodorization will take place after cleaning, too.

All clothing will have to be deodorized during laundry and dry cleaning and, in serious cases, will be put in an ozone room that opens the oxygen molecules and releases odor.

Ozone machines are also used for deodorizing the home, resulting in a smell much like the air after a thunderstorm.

The best deodorization technique I have ever known is to re-create the conditions causing the odor. In the case of smoke damage, a deodorant "smoke" is produced, which penetrates in exactly the same manner the smoke odor did.

Additional odor control is done with duct sealing and deodorization.

Additionally, all walls that are washed and to be painted should be sealed first with a special sealer to eliminate residue "bleed through" from the oily smoke film. Then the walls are painted in the normal manner. Your disaster restoration firm and adjuster will be familiar with this process.

With light smoke damage, many times the wall-washing is necessary, but not painting. Deodorization is generally always advised.

WHAT IF YOU DON'T HAVE INSURANCE?

The best advice I can give you is to carry insurance. If you live in an apartment or condominium, buy renter's insurance. If smoke damage occurs, you'll be glad you did.

But if you don't have insurance, here's some helpful advice:

Go to a janitorial supply store and ask their advice on which cleaning chemicals to use. They can provide you with a professional-quality deodorant to wash clothes, linens, and hard surfaces. You will put this deodorant in the water that you clean with or wash clothes with.

Call a disaster restoration firm and try to rent an ozone machine to deodorize the structure and your contents, bearing in mind that prolonged ozone exposure will yellow plastics.

Buy a soot-and-dirt-removal sponge to clean walls. This is somewhat like a blackboard eraser that removes oily smoke film, so that when you begin to wash the walls, the sooty film won't smear.

Rent a carpet-cleaning machine with an upholstery attachment to clean carpet and all upholstery that can be cleaned with water.

Wash hard furniture with oil soap and dry, then use furniture polish if you want a brighter shine.

WASH EVERYTHING

Wash everything thoroughly—this means walls, cupboards, collectibles, dishes, clothes, etc.—otherwise the odor will remain.

Start in one room and do it completely except for carpet cleaning (you'll track during the cleaning and spread soot on the carpet). Clean the carpet in all rooms last.

If you still have odor, do a final deodorization with an ozone machine or, if you can, hire a firm to come in and do it for you.

31

THE BIG DRIP—
WATER DAMAGE
RESTORATION

What a shock! When you left the house everything was fine.

You come home and unlock the door; you walk in and hear the sound of running water. As you step in, water comes up to your ankles. Now you find water running across the carpet and floors and lapping at the legs of furniture as the sofa and chairs try to soak it up. Here's what you need to do immediately.

TURN IT OFF

First, know where your water shutoff is and use it. Turn off the water and look for the source of the leak. BE SURE THE ELECTRICAL POWER SOURCE IS OFF BEFORE YOU WALK IN STANDING WATER. The leak could be from a toilet, the washing machine hoses, or a broken pipe.

How quickly you react will have an impact on what can be saved in your home.

CALL THE PROFESSIONALS

Now that you have shut off the water and located the problem, call your insurance agent. Your agent will act quickly to help you, because by the time an adjuster receives the information, it is often too late to reverse some of the damage that has taken place.

Wet carpet and pad are restorable if they are taken care of as soon as possible after the damage has occurred.

A professional company that deals in water damage of all kinds can stop further damage from occurring and also save the carpet and pad.

To find a water damage expert, look in the yellow pages under "water damage" or under "cleaning companies" or "disaster restoration firms." Be sure to get a company that specializes in this problem.

DRY OUT

First they will extract water from the pad and the carpet and treat both with an EPA-registered disinfectant. They will then install drying equipment, which consists of high-powered carpet blowers that are slipped between the carpet and the pad. They also will install dehumidification equipment to facilitate drying. They will advise you to keep your home's interior temperature at 70 degrees or warmer for ideal drying conditions. This equipment will also facilitate drying of upholstered furniture and walls as it dries the carpet.

Upholstered furniture will need to have water extracted from it and to be treated with an EPA-registered disinfectant, too. Wood furniture will be wiped down and allowed to dry.

The water damage restoration firm will check, usually

SEWER BACKUPS

If your water damage is due to a sewer backup, disaster restoration firms are trained to deal with it. Stay out of the water and waste. Let the trained experts deal with the water and bacterial problems; that's their job and they know what can be saved and what can't.

every 24 hours, to see how the drying is coming along and to move equipment to continue the drying.

WHAT IS AN ANTIMICROBIAL?

Many water damage restoration firms have a wonderful antimicrobial product available that not only disinfects, but also inhibits the growth of mold, mildew, and bacterial spores. This is applied to the carpet after water extraction takes place and has certainly saved many a carpet.

After all the carpets and contents of your home are dry, the upholstery and carpet will be cleaned and again treated with a disinfectant or antimicrobial. Hard furniture will be washed and polished, and hard floors will be given a final cleaning. If your carpet or upholstery had a protective coating on it, this will be reapplied.

Walls will be washed as needed and your home will be returned to normal once again.

ANSWERS TO YOUR SEA OF WORRIES

The Pad Will Dissolve!

Not so! Most pads are made of non-water-sensitive foam bonded with a dry solvent-soluble adhesive.

The Seams Will Separate!

Now that is logical. Wet carpet naturally means shrinkage, right? WRONG! Non-water-soluble adhesives are used on seams. Regardless of what happens, seams can be repaired.

The Carpet Will Shrink off the Wall!

Only poorly installed carpet will come loose from the wall, and this is easily restretched.

The Carpet Will Fall Apart!

This is not likely. Carpet manufacturers actually immerse carpet in water many times during its dyeing and rinsing. Synthetic fibers, the primary backings, and latex adhesives are virtually unaffected by water for at least 48 hours.

32

TAKING THE ACHOO OUT OF YOUR AIR DUCTS

Picture yourself in this situation: You have had smoke damage in your home. All the cleaning and repainting is done, and now you are ready to turn on the furnace. You go to the thermostat and turn it up. You hear the furnace spring to life. The central blower is activated . . . and, suddenly, you run screaming from the house. What's wrong? All the odor that collected in the duct system during the smoke damage has just been blown full force from the duct system and into the house. It smells like the house is on fire again. As if the smell isn't enough, you now see black soot residue blowing out in a dark cloud and settling all over the newly cleaned walls, carpet, and furniture. How could this happen? Nobody thought to clean the duct system prior to cleaning the house and turning on the furnace.

Duct cleaning and deodorizing is not just for houses that have had fire or smoke damage. In older homes, dust and allergy-causing bacteria may have accumulated in the ductwork and be blown through the home each time the furnace runs. Duct cleaning can be very beneficial, too, for people who have allergy problems.

FRESH AIR
You've had smoke damage . . . you have allergies . . . you just purchased an older home. . . . This is some healthy advice for cleaner air and a fresher smell.

WHAT IS DUCT CLEANING?

Duct cleaning consists of removing register covers and vacuuming out all the ductwork that leads to the furnace. After some elaborate preparatory vacuuming and cleaning, which includes cleaning all the register covers, a duct sealer is introduced into the system in the form of a fine mist. This sealer is a plasticlike resin. The chemical neutralizes odor and seals onto the interior walls of the system the loose soot, dust, and dirt that remain after vacuuming. This eliminates all odor, and minor residues remaining in unseen or unreachable areas are permanently sealed onto the interior surface of the ducts.

This gives you a dirt-, dust-, and pollen-free environment. If allergies run in your family, you will immediately notice the difference. This is particularly good in older homes that, naturally, have the original duct systems in place.

When you have this procedure done, it is a good idea to have your furnace cleaned at the same time. Many furnace companies clean ductwork, too, as do many disaster restoration or cleaning companies.

33

STOP THE SCIENCE EXPERIMENT— MOLD AND MILDEW

L eft unchecked, dampness in a home or basement can rot wood, peel paint, and promote rust and mildew.

FIND THE SOURCE

Here is a simple test to determine if dampness is caused by seepage or excessive humidity:

Cut several 12-inch squares of aluminum foil. Tape them in various spots on the floor and walls; seal the edges tightly. If moisture collects between the foil and the surface after several days, waterproof the interior walls. If moisture forms on the foil's surface, take the following steps:

- Close windows on humid days.
- Install a window exhaust fan.
- Vent your clothes dryer to the outside.
- Use a dehumidifier, especially during summer months.
- Treat walls with epoxy-based waterproofing paint or masonry sealer. (To clean walls in preparation for paint, look for special mildew cleaners in home centers.)

MAKE YOUR OWN TREATMENT

You can also make your own mildew treatment by mixing a quart of chlorine bleach and a tablespoon of powdered nonammoniated laundry detergent with 3 quarts of warm water. Scrub the mildew-stained surface with the solution and allow it to work until the discoloration vanishes, rinse thoroughly, and allow to dry.

Caution

Be sure to wear goggles, rubber gloves, and protective clothing when using this solution. Never allow it to come

in contact with carpet or fabrics, and clean the shoes you wear before walking on carpets. Do this in a well-ventilated area.

SUMMERTIME TIPS

Mold can become a serious problem in homes. Balmy summer weather promotes outdoor activity and indoor activity, too. It is the prime time for mold and mildew growth.

For small children and the elderly and allergy and asthma sufferers, mold can trigger a wide variety of symptoms, including irritation and even sinus and respiratory infections. Here are some specific summertime tips to help you avoid the mold invasion:

- Clean soap scum and soil off bathroom walls and fixtures.
- Turn on vent fans prior to showering.
- Wipe excess moisture off shower walls.
- Check for mold growing around windows and door entries.
- If you have water damage in your home, contact a professional or follow careful cleaning and drying procedures.
- Be sure water drains away from your home foundation.

- Take moisture problems in the basement seriously and contact a professional if necessary.
- When cleaning surfaces with mold and mildew, use disinfectants or products labeled "mildew removers."
- Fix household leaks promptly.

RESOURCE GUIDE

ACT NATURAL® CLOTHS: These microfiber cloths and mops clean and disinfect without chemicals, using only water. They have been scientifically proven to kill germs and bacteria and even come with a warranty. They are easy to use, great for people with allergies, and can be cleaned and sanitized in the washer (this is particularly important with the mop). Use them in the kitchen, bathroom, to spot carpet, on windows, mirrors, hard furniture, in the car—virtually anywhere you clean. Call 888-638-2882 or visit www.act-natural.net. They are a wonderful investment. My mop is five years old and is still doing the job.

ART GUM ERASER: You remember the little brownish-tan, rectangular eraser that you used in school, the one that crumbled as you erased? That's the one!

BAKING POWDER: If you bake, you already have this in the cupboard. If not, look in the baking section near the baking soda. Baking powder and baking soda are not the same thing, so don't even go there!

BEESWAX: Is usually found in drugstores, hardware stores, and natural-product stores. If you don't see it, ask!

BITTER APPLE: This keeps pets from dining on your plants, etc. It is not harmful to them, but tastes terrible, so it discourages them entirely. Look for it at pet supply stores.

BORAX: Better known as 20 Mule Team® Borax, this laundry additive can be found in the detergent aisle.

BRUCE® FLOOR CARE PRODUCTS: Look for these products at hardware stores, home centers, and wherever wood flooring is sold. You can also find information at www.florstor.com.

CALGON® WATER SOFTENER: Look for it with the laundry additives at the grocery store.

CHAMOIS: Found in hardware stores and home centers.

CHARCOAL: This is the type made for fish tanks and is available at pet supply stores.

CLEAR AMMONIA: There are two types of ammonia, clear and sudsy. Clear contains no soap and should be used where suggested for that reason.

COLD CREAM: Plain old Pond's® that your grandma used on her face, or the store brand.

CUTICLE REMOVER: The gel you apply to your cuticles to soften them. Let's be clear, it is cuticle remover, *not* nail polish remover.

DENATURED ALCOHOL: This is an industrial alcohol reserved for heavy-duty cleaning. Don't use it near open flame, and dispose outside the home any rags that were used to apply it. Launder or clean as soon as possible anything that you treat with it. Look for this in cans at hardware stores and home centers. Remember the Queen's rule: always test in an inconspicuous place before treating a large area with this product.

FELS-NAPTHA® LAUNDRY BAR SOAP: What a wonderful laundry spotter and cleaner this is. You'll find it in the bar-soap section of the grocery store. It's usually on the bottom shelf in a small stack and always has dust on it, because nobody knows what to use it for.

FINE DRYWALL SANDPAPER: This sandpaper looks like window screen. Make sure you buy a package marked "fine grade."

FINE STEEL WOOL: Look for the symbol 0000 and the word *fine*. And don't try soap-filled steel-wool pads. They are not acceptable substitutes.

GLYCERIN: Look for glycerin in drugstores in the hand cream section. Always purchase plain glycerin, not the type containing rose water.

GOJO® CRÈME WATERLESS HAND CLEANER: People with greasy hands have used this product for years. It's a hand cleaner and so much more. Look for it at home centers and hardware stores.

HYDROGEN PEROXIDE: Choose the type that you use on cuts and to gargle with—not the type used to bleach hair. That will remove color from carpet or fabric.

LEATHER CPR™: This miracle product conditions and cleans all types of leather, except suede. Totally neutral, Leather CPR™ can be used on leather furniture, car upholstery, purses, shoes, and equestrian equipment—and on any color leather. It is without a doubt the best leather cleaner I have ever found. Check www.leathercpr.com to order or for a store location near you.

LEMON OR ORANGE EXTRACT: These are found in the spice area of the grocery store where vanilla extract is located.

LINSEED OIL: You'll find this at the hardware store, usually in the paint and staining section. It is combustible, so use care in disposing of rags or paper towels used to apply it. Keep it in the garage or basement away from open flame.

MEAT TENDERIZER: Use the unseasoned variety please, or you will have a whole new stain to deal with. Store brands work fine.

NAIL POLISH REMOVER: I caution you to use nonacetone polish remover, which is much less aggressive than acetone polish remover. (Straight acetone is exceedingly strong.) Use only where recommended and with great care. Look for this product at beauty supply stores.

NATURAL SPONGE: A natural sponge is the best sponge you will ever use. It has hundreds of natural "scrubbing fingers" that make any wall-washing job speed by. Look for these at home centers and hardware stores and choose a nice size to fit your hand. Wash them in lukewarm water with gentle suds. You can put them in the washing machine if you avoid combining them with fabrics that have lint.

NONGEL TOOTHPASTE: This is just a fancy name for old-fashioned plain white toothpaste. Gels just don't work, so don't even try.

ODORZOUT®: A fabulous, dry, 100 percent natural deodorizer. It's nontoxic, so you can use it anyplace you have a smell or a stink. It is especially effective on pet urine odors, and since it is used dry, it is simple to apply. Call 800-88STINK, or visit their website at www.88stink.com.

OIL OF CLOVES: Widely available at health food stores, vitamin stores, and natural food stores.

POWDERED ALUM: This old-fashioned product was once used in pickling. Look for it at drugstores, and if you can't find it, ask the pharmacist.

RED ERASE™: Removes kids' red stains. Call 888-WINEAWAY.

ROTTENSTONE: Mild pumice; look for it at hardware stores and home centers.

RUST REMOVER: These are serious products, so follow the directions carefully. Look for products like Whink® and Rust Magic® at hardware stores and home centers.

SADDLE SOAP: You will find this in the hardware store or in the shoe polish section at most any store.

SHAVING CREAM: The cheaper brands work fine, and shaving cream works better than gel.

SOOT-AND-DIRT-REMOVAL SPONGE: These are used to clean walls, wallpaper, lampshades, and even soot. They also remove pet hair from upholstery. These big brick erasers are available at home centers and hardware stores, usually near the wallpaper supplies. Clean them by washing in a pail of warm water and liquid dish soap, rinse well, and allow to dry before using again.

SQUEEGEE: When buying a squeegee for washing windows, look for a good-quality one with a replaceable rubber blade. For best results, always be sure that the rubber blade is soft and flexible. Look for these at hardware stores, home centers, and janitorial supply companies. They come in different widths, so be sure to think about the size windows, etc., that you are going to use it for. A 12-inch blade is a good starting point.

TACK-TRAP®: Bugs are drawn to the color of this sticky sheet. Sold in garden supply stores and some hardware stores.

TANG® BREAKFAST DRINK: Yes, this is the product that the astronauts took to the moon! It is also a great cleaner. (Store brands work just as well.)

TRISODIUM PHOSPHATE (TSP): Cleaning professionals have used this product for years. It is wonderful for washing walls, garage floors, and for any tough cleaning job. Look for it at hardware stores, home centers, and janitorial supply stores. Wear rubber gloves when using it.

TYPEWRITER ERASER: A thing of the past, but still available at office supply stores. Shaped like a pencil with a little brush where the pencil eraser would be, it can be sharpened like a pencil and will last for years.

WASHING SODA: I like Arm and Hammer® Washing Soda, which can be found in the detergent aisle at the grocery store along with other laundry additives. No, you cannot substitute baking soda, it is a different product!

WAX CRAYONS: These are sold in hardware stores and home centers and come in various wood colors for concealing scratches in wood surfaces. Don't be fooled by the color name; try to take along a sample of what you need to patch to get the best possible match.

WD-40® LUBRICANT: I bet you will find a can in your garage or basement. Fine spray oil for lubricating all kinds of things, it's a wonderful product for regenerating grease so that it can be removed from clothes. Look for WD-40® at the hardware store, home center, and even the grocery store.

WHITING: Look for this at the hardware store, usually near the paint.

WINDOW SCRUBBER: This looks like a squeegee wearing a coat. Look for it at janitorial supply stores and home centers.

WINE AWAY® RED WINE STAIN REMOVER: This unbelievable product can remove red stains, such as red wine, red pop, cranberry juice, red food coloring, grape juice, etc., from carpet and fabric. It is totally nontoxic and made from fruit and vegetable extracts. I just can't believe how well it works! Look for it where liquor is sold or call 888-WINEAWAY for a store location near you.

WINTERGREEN OIL: Widely available at health food stores, natural food stores, and some linen stores.

ZUD® HEAVY DUTY CLEANSER: This is a wonderful cleanser for really tough jobs. It works great on rust on hard surfaces, too. Find it at hardware stores, home centers, and grocery stores. Well worth keeping on hand.

INDEX

Acid soot residue, 192–93
ACT Natural® Microfiber Cloths, 21, 31, 64, 125, 211
ACT Natural® Mop, 64, 66
Air cleaners, 125–27
Air ducts, 203–05; cleaning, 204–05; fire damage, 203–04
Air fresheners, 34
Allergies, 31, 33, 43; duct cleaning, 204, 205; dust mites, 126; mold, 208
Almond oil, 26, 81
Aluminum: baked-enamel finish, 153–54; cleaner, 27; patio furniture, 153–54
Aluminum foil, 7, 24, 28, 50, 148, 165, 207
Ammonia, clear, 98, 99, 104, 148, 172, 173, 212; for bathroom cleaning, 4, 9, 62; for kitchen cleaning, 13, 14, 20, 21, 24, 27; for wall-washing, 85–86
Answering machine, 135
Antimicrobial products, 201
Ants, 181–82
Aphids, 182–83
Appliances: marker stains, 116; instructions, 19; white, cleaning, 11–13, 40

Artificial flowers, cleaning, 178–79
Asthma, 31, 43, 208
Athlete's foot, 188

Baby oil, 26, 82
Baked-enamel finish, aluminum with, 153–54
Baking powder, 211–12
Baking soda, 4, 35–37, 74, 99, 106, 109, 113, 114, 119, 122, 135, 164, 165, 171, 183, 187; for bathroom cleaning, 4, 6, 35–37; for kitchen cleaning, 12, 13, 16, 17, 20, 21, 22, 25, 27, 35–37; for laundry, 35, 36, 37; for odor control, 35–37; uses of, 35–37; for wall-washing, 84–86
Bandage removal, 113
Bank safe-deposit box, 192
Bar soap, 52, 80, 149, 166, 172
Basil, 184
Bathing children, 112
Bathroom, 1–10; chrome faucet cleaning, 6; decal removal, 7; Fiberglas™ shower and tub, 2, 3; glass shower door soap scum removal, 5, 33; hair spray residue removal, 6, 9–10; hard-water mark removal, 3; marble, 96–100;

 **Your Personal Tips and Hints**

👑 Your Personal Tips and Hints 👑

Own the Complete Library of
QUEEN OF CLEAN® Books

ADDED VALUE!

Enjoy these helpful hints from
*THE ROYAL GUIDE
TO SPOT AND STAIN
REMOVAL*

Don't get mad, get clean!

ADHESIVE TAPE: Sponge adhesive tape with eucalyptus oil, baby oil, or cooking oil. Allow to soak 10 minutes or so, then work in undiluted dishwashing liquid and rinse well. Pretreat and launder as usual.

You may also consider using De-Solv-It™, Goo Gone™, or Un-Du™ to remove adhesives from fabric and hard surfaces. Un-Du™ is so great it will remove a stamp from an envelope!

ALCOHOLIC BEVERAGES: These stains will turn brown with age, so it is important to treat them as soon as possible. First, flush the area with cold water or with club soda, then sponge immediately with a cloth barely dampened with warm water and 1 or 2 drops of liquid dish soap. Rinse with cool water and dry the area with a hair dryer set on medium.

Alcohol is often invisible when it is spilled, but it can oxidize with heat and age, which makes it impossible to remove. Presoak dry alcohol stains in an enzyme solution such as Biz® All Fabric Bleach, and launder as usual.

If you spill alcohol on a dry-clean-only fabric, sponge with cold water or club soda and then take the garment to the dry cleaner as soon as possible. Make sure to point out the stain.

For beer spills, sponge with a solution of equal parts white vinegar and dishwashing liquid, then rinse in warm water.

ANIMAL HAIR: Removing pet hair from clothes and bedding can be a challenge. Try using a damp sponge and wiping over clothes and bedding, etc. Rinse the sponge frequently to keep it clean. You can also remove hair by putting on rubber gloves and dipping them in water. Simply dip and wipe, dip and wipe. The hair will rinse off easily.

BABY FORMULA: For white clothes, try applying lemon juice to the stains and laying the garment in the sun. Pretreat and launder as usual.

Unseasoned meat tenderizer is also great for removing formula and baby food stains. Make a paste of the tenderizer and cool water, rub it into the stain, and let sit for an hour or so before laundering. Meat tenderizer contains an enzyme that breaks down protein stains. Just make sure to use *unseasoned* tenderizer.

Soaking colored clothes and whites in Brilliant Bleach® is also effective, although you may have to soak for several days to achieve perfect results on difficult stains. Remember, this bleach is nonchlorine, so it's totally safe for baby things.

BERRIES (blueberries, cranberries, raspberries, strawberries): There are many complex ways to deal with berry stains, but I've had great success with one of the simplest, a product called Wine Away® Red Wine Stain Remover. Don't be fooled by the name, it works on red fruit stains and juices too.

Just spray Wine Away® straight on the fabric and watch in amazement as it breaks down the stain. Follow the directions on the container carefully and launder immediately after use. Totally nontoxic, Wine Away® is safe on all washable surfaces.

BEVERAGES: Blot beverage spills immediately until you have absorbed all you can, then sponge with clean, warm water and a little borax. (About ½ teaspoon borax to ½ cup of water.) Sponge and blot repeatedly and launder as usual.

BLOOD (fresh and dried): If you have blood all over your clothes, laundry may not be your biggest problem . . . for those little accidents try the following:

For washable fabrics, soak as soon as possible in salt water or flush with club soda. You can also make a paste of unseasoned meat tenderizer and cold water, and apply it to the stain for a few hours. Wash in cool water and detergent, by hand or machine.

Pouring 3 percent hydrogen peroxide through the stained area can be effective in many instances. The sooner you do this the more success you will have. Make sure to do this only on washable fabrics, please. Pour the peroxide through the stain, then flush with cold water, pretreat and launder as usual.

Biz® All Fabric Bleach and Brilliant Bleach® both work well on blood. When using Biz®, make a paste with cold water and apply to the stain, allowing it to sit for several hours. With Brilliant Bleach®, soak the garment for a significant period of time—anywhere between 1 to 24 hours. Neither of these products will harm colorfast fabrics.

For dry-clean-only fabrics, sprinkle with salt while the blood is still moist, then take to a dry cleaner as soon as possible.

Human saliva will break down fresh bloodstains, so try applying a little of your own saliva to a small spot of blood—this may do the trick.

For a quick fix for fresh bloodstains, apply cornstarch to the surface and then flush from the "wrong" side of the fabric with soapy water. Pretreat and launder as usual.

Blood on leather can be foamed away with 3 percent hydrogen peroxide. Dab on the peroxide. Let it bubble and then blot. Continue until the blood is removed. Wipe the surface with a damp cloth and dry.

COFFEE AND TEA (black or with sugar): Blot up all that you can and, if the garment is washable, flush immediately with cold water. Rub detergent into the stain and work well between your thumbs before laundering as usual. If the stain is still visible and you can use hot water on the fabric, spread the stain over the sink, or stretch over a bowl and tie or rubber band in place (like a little trampoline), and set the bowl in the sink. Cover the stain with 20 Mule Team® Borax and pour boiling water through it, circling from the outside of the stain until you have reached the center. Let soak 30 minutes to an hour and relaunder.

For sturdy whites, such as knits and T-shirts, dissolve 2

denture-cleaning tablets in warm water and soak the stain for 30 minutes. Check the garment. If the stain is still visible, soak again and launder as usual.

Out at a restaurant? Dip your napkin in water and sprinkle with salt and blot the offending stain.

COLLAR STAINS: This is for those women whose husbands won't share laundry duty, the women who didn't know that the wedding ring came with a ring around the collar! It's easy to remove, though. Just use some inexpensive shampoo! Shampoo dissolves body oils so it works great on that collar ring. Keep some in a bottle with a dispenser top in the laundry room. Squirt on enough to cover the offending stain and work it in well, then launder as usual.

CRAYON AND COLORED PENCIL: Place the stained area on a pad of paper towels and spray with WD-40® Lubricant. Let stand for a few minutes, then turn the fabric over and spray the other side. Let sit for a further 10 minutes before working undiluted dishwashing liquid into the stained area to remove the crayon and oil. Replace the paper-toweling pad as necessary. Wash in the hottest possible water for the fabric, along with your normal detergent and appropriate bleaching agent (depending on whether the clothes are white or colored). Wash on the longest wash cycle available, and rinse well.

Another way to remove crayon from washable fabrics such as wool, acrylic, linen, cotton and polyester is to lay the offending stain between two pieces of brown paper and press with a warm/medium iron. A grocery bag works well—just remember to keep any ink that may be on the bag away from the fabric. The paper works as a blotter to absorb the crayon, so keep changing it as the wax is absorbed. If any color mark remains, soak the garment in Brilliant Bleach®.

Note: Don't panic if the crayon has also gone through

the dryer. Simply spray an old rag with WD-40® Lubricant; then thoroughly wipe down the drum. Make sure the dryer is empty when you do this—no clothes, no crayons. Place a load of dry rags in the dryer and run through a drying cycle when you're through. This will remove any oily residue.

DYE: Dye stains are difficult if not impossible to remove. Try one or all of these methods.

Spread the stained area over a bowl and put a rubber band around the fabric *and* the bowl to hold the fabric taut, like a trampoline. Set the bowl in the sink with the drain in the open position to allow the water to run freely away. Turn on the cold water faucet to a nice steady drip and let it drip through the dye spot for 3 to 6 hours. Monitor the sink to be sure the water is draining. This treatment is effective in many cases.

You can also try saturating the dye spot with a combination of equal parts 3 percent hydrogen peroxide and water. Set the fabric in the sun, keeping it moist with the solution until the spot completely disappears. Rinse well and launder as usual. Use only on colorfast clothes.

If your dye problem is caused from fugitive color—that is, color that has run from one fabric to another during the wash cycle—all the bleaching in the world won't help. Try Synthrapol™ or Carbona Color Run Remover™ instead.

Quilters have used Synthrapol™ for years to remove color that runs in homemade quilts. Make sure to read *all* the directions on the bottle prior to using.

Carbona Color Run Remover™ is extremely effective on cotton fabrics. It is not for delicates or some blends, so do read the box with care. It may also cause damage to buttons and, in some cases, zippers. You may want to remove these prior to treating.

EGG: First scrape off any solid matter. Then, soak the fabric in a glass or plastic container with any enzyme-soaking product, such as Biz® Non Chlorine Bleach. Soak for at least 6 hours or overnight. If a stain remains, work in powder detergent, rubbing vigorously between your thumbs. Rinse and wash as usual. Check the garment carefully for any remaining stain when you remove it from the washer. Don't apply heat until all of the stain is removed or the stain will become permanent.

You can also try treating the area with cool water and unseasoned meat tenderizer. Work this into the area well, and allow it to sit for a few hours, being sure to keep the area moist. Continue treating until no stain remains.

Take nonwashables to the dry cleaner as soon as possible. Quick treatment is important. Make sure you identify the stain to your cleaner so it can be treated properly and promptly.

FOOD DYE: Fruit juices, gelatin desserts, fruit smoothies, and frozen fruit sticks all contain food dye that can leave a nasty stain on clothes.

Treating the stain while it is still fresh is the very best thing you can do. If you are out in public and don't have access to any cleaning supplies, wet the spot with club soda or cool water and blot, blot, blot. If you are at home, then treat the spot with 1 cup of cool water to which you have added 1 tablespoon of ammonia. Once you have flushed the spot well with this solution, grab the salt shaker and rub salt into the wound . . . I mean stain! Let this sit for an hour or so, and then brush off the salt. If the stain is still visible, re-treat the same way.

You can also try stretching the fabric tight and holding it under a forceful stream of cold water. This will flush out much of the spot without spreading it. Next, rub in your favorite detergent, scrubbing vigorously between your thumbs. Rinse again in cool water. Do not apply heat to the stain until it is completely removed.

I have had great success soaking food dye spills in Brilliant Bleach® (follow the directions for hand-soaking on the container).

If you are dealing with a red, orange, or purple stain, try Wine Away® Red Wine Stain Remover, used according to directions. Don't be fooled by the name—it is great for all red-type stains. You will be amazed!

Remember, if the stain is not removed during the spotting process, it will not come out in the laundry!

FURNITURE POLISH: Furniture polish is usually an oil-based stain, so it must be reconstituted. Restore the oil in the polish by spraying with WD-40® Lubricant. Allow the lubricant to soak for 10 minutes, then work in undiluted dishwashing liquid. Work this in well between your thumbs to remove the grease. Flush with a forceful stream of the hottest water you can for the fabric type. Pretreat with a product such as Zout®, which is great for grease spots, and launder as usual.

GRASS, FLOWERS AND FOLIAGE: There are several ways to remove grass stains from fabrics. Pick one and try it. If it doesn't completely remove the stain, try another. Don't put clothes into the dryer until the grass stain is removed.

First a word of caution: Avoid using alkalis such as ammonia, degreasers or alkaline detergents. They interact with the tannin in the grass stains and may permanently set the stain.

Okay—first, washable fabrics: Sponge on rubbing alcohol, repeating several times. If the stain persists, sponge with white vinegar and rinse. Work in your favorite laundry detergent and rinse well.

Rubbing white nongel toothpaste into grass stains will often remove them. Rub well, then rinse and wash as usual.

For jeans, apply undiluted alcohol to the area and allow to soak 15 minutes before laundering as usual.

Zout® also works very well on grass stains. Follow the label directions. Biz® All Fabric Bleach made into a paste with cold water is effective in treating stubborn grass stains too.

For grass on white leather shoes, rub the grass stain with molasses and leave it on the shoe overnight. Wash the molasses off with hot soap and water, and the grass stain should be gone.

For grass on suede fabric, including shoes, rub the stain with a sponge dipped in glycerin. Then rub with a cloth dipped in undiluted white vinegar, brush the nap gently to reset, and allow to dry and brush again. Remember: test in an inconspicuous spot first.

INK: How can one little pen cause so much grief? The first line of offense is rubbing alcohol. Sponge the ink mark, or dip it into a glass of rubbing alcohol, letting it soak until the offending spot is removed. Don't be tricked into using hair spray. That may have worked in the past, but hair spray now contains a lot of oil, and that just spreads the stain.

Denatured alcohol—a much stronger version of rubbing alcohol—may be more effective. Test this first in an inconspicuous spot, as denatured alcohol may damage some fabrics.

You also can try using acetone. This too must be tested. (And remember, *never* use acetone on acetates.)

White, nongel toothpaste rubbed firmly and vigorously into the stain may work. After this method be sure to pretreat and launder as usual.

Often just soaking ink stains in milk will dissolve them.

Turpentine is effective on very challenging ink stains. Working over a pad of paper towels, tap the spot on the back of the fabric using the back of a spoon or an old toothbrush. Don't rub. Work in undiluted dishwashing liquid prior to laundering, and wash in the hottest water possible for the fabric type. Dispose of all paper, etc., saturated with turpentine immediately—outside, please.

KOOL-AID®: Flush the spot as quickly as possible with club soda and then hold under forceful running water. If a stained area still remains, soak in Brilliant Bleach® until the stain is removed. This may take hours or days, depending on the fabric and the stain. Soak only white or colorfast clothes in Brilliant Bleach®.

LIPSTICK: Lipstick is actually an oily dye stain. Water, heat or wet spotters will only spread it and make the problem worse and set the stain.

Rub in vegetable oil, WD-40® Lubricant or mineral oil and let it sit on the spot for 15 to 30 minutes. Next sponge the area with a little ammonia—sudsy or clear is fine.

Now, before you launder, work in undiluted liquid dish soap to be sure you have removed all of the oil.

Another method I have had real success with is GOJO® Crème Waterless Hand Cleaner. Look for this at hardware stores and home centers. Work it into the lipstick, rubbing between your thumbs vigorously. Launder as usual. This method is great for the smear of lipstick on cloth table napkins.

In an emergency, try spraying the spot with a little hair spray. Let this sit for a few minutes and then wipe gently with a damp cloth. Test this method in an inconspicuous spot first.

You will also find that Zout® and Whink Wash Away Laundry Spotter™ are generally effective on lipstick.

For really stubborn, old stains, try moistening with denatured alcohol, then treat with undiluted liquid dish soap.

If you are getting dressed and you accidentally get lipstick on your clothes, try rubbing the stain with white bread. (Yes, it has to be white!)

MAKEUP (oily foundation, powder, cream blush, cover creams): Sprinkle baking soda on the makeup smudge, then brush the area with an old wet toothbrush until the makeup is removed. Nongel white toothpaste scrubbed with a toothbrush is also effective.

Liquid dish soap or shampoo will generally remove makeup stains. Work the product into the stain vigorously between your thumbs.

For stubborn makeup stains use nonoily makeup remover, pretreat and launder as usual.

MUD: The key word here is *dry*. Let mud dry. Never treat a wet mud stain other than lifting off any solid pieces with a dull straightedge. Once mud has dried, take the vacuum cleaner and vacuum the area with the hose attachment. You'll achieve the greatest suction that way. This may be a two-person job: one to hold the fabric, one to hold the hose.

Rub the cut side of a potato over the mud stain and launder as usual.

For stubborn stains, sponge with equal portions of rubbing alcohol and cool water. For red mud stains, treat with a rust remover. Rubbing 20 Mule Team® Borax into a dampened mud stain will often remove it.

MYSTERY STAINS: These are spots and spills that you have no idea where they came from. The unknowns. Here's what to do:

• Blot with cool water (hot water sets stains).

• Blot with a sponge or cloth dampened with water and a teaspoon or so of white vinegar (not for cotton or linen).

• Blot with a sponge or cloth dampened with water and a teaspoon or so of clear ammonia (again, not for cotton or linen).

• Blot with rubbing alcohol diluted 50/50 with cool water.

• Sponge with a solution of Brilliant Bleach® and water.

NAIL POLISH: Okay, if you had polished your nails naked in the backyard you wouldn't be reading this, would you? Stretch the fabric over a glass bowl and make a little trampoline by securing the fabric with a rubber band. Drip acetone-based polish remover through the stain with a stainless steel spoon (not silver) and tap the stain with the edge of the spoon. Continue dripping the acetone through the fabric until the polish is removed. This requires time and patience. If you run out of either, walk away and come back later. Straight acetone, purchased at the hardware store or beauty supply, may work faster, but be sure to test an area first.

If a color stain remains after the polish is removed, dilute hydrogen peroxide (50 percent peroxide, 50 percent water), apply to the stain, and set the fabric in the sun, keeping it moist with the peroxide solution. Do this only for white or colorfast clothes.

Do not use acetone on silk or acetates, and always test the acetone on an inconspicuous area prior to beginning.

Nonwashable fabrics should be dry-cleaned.

ODORS: Eliminate odors, don't use a perfumed cover-up. I like ODORZOUT® odor eliminator because it absorbs odors and removes them permanently—without leaving any telltale smells behind. It is nontoxic and safe for all surfaces, and it can be used wet or dry. It is also safe for the environment and a little goes a long way. Keep some on hand. It's great for just about any odor you're likely to come across, such as smoke, mildew, mold, feces, urine, food odors, any kind of odor. Do not use a perfumed cover-up.

OINTMENT (A and D ointment, Desitin, zinc oxide): Anyone who has had a baby will be familiar with this problem stain. Use hot water and detergent, rubbing the fabric against itself to remove the oil. For zinc oxide, soak the garment in white vinegar for 30 minutes after treating as above, then launder as usual.

PAINT, LATEX: Treat this stain immediately for best results. It is important to remove paint *before* it dries, so keep the stain wet if you can't work on it right away.

Flush the paint from the fabric with a forceful stream of warm water. Next, treat the stain with a solution of liquid dish soap and water, or laundry detergent and water. Work it into the stained area, soaping and rinsing until the stain is removed. Do this as many times as necessary. If the fabric is colorfast, you can also work in some automatic dishwasher detergent and let it soak on the fabric for 5 to 10 minutes before laundering as usual.

You can also try a product aptly named OOPS!™ Just follow the directions on the can closely.

On fabrics such as cotton and polyester, try spraying the garment with oven cleaner and letting it sit about 15 to 30 minutes before flushing with plenty of water. Use *extreme* care with this method and use it at your own risk. Some fabrics cannot tolerate the oven cleaner, but if the garment is ruined by the paint, it is worth a try. Also use care where you spray the oven cleaner and what you set the fabric on afterward.

PAINT, OIL-BASED: Get busy and remove this spill ASAP. You're out of luck if it dries. If you must go to the store for products, keep the spill moist: *Do not allow oil-based paint to dry.*

Check the paint can and use the thinner recommended by the manufacturer. Sometimes thinner for correction fluid will also work. Remember to test an area first with these two methods.

I fall back on turpentine when all else fails. Work the turpentine into the spill, and once the paint is removed, work in GOJO® Crème Waterless Hand Cleaner. That will take out the oiliness from the turpentine. Remember to dispose of turpentine soaked rags or paper towels outside, as soon as possible.

When working on a paint spill, work from the back of the fabric over a thick pad of paper towels. Tap the stained area with an old toothbrush or an old spoon as you work to force the paint out.

Now that you have removed the stain, saturate it with detergent and work in vigorously. Cover the area with the hottest water you can use for the fabric, and let it soak overnight. Scrub again, between your thumbs, and launder as usual.

PENCIL: Okay, how easy is this? Take a nice, clean, soft eraser, and gently rub the offending mark away! Just be sure the eraser is clean, or you will create a large stain.

PERFUME: Follow the directions in the section on *Alcoholic Beverages.* A few words to the wise: The best time to put it on is right before you put on your clothes, not after. And never spray perfume directly on your clothes. This will damage them. The combination of alcohol and oil is death to fabrics.

PERSPIRATION STAINS: These stains are really the pits. Perspiration will weaken fabrics, so treat vulnerable areas with care and treat those invisible perspiration problems right after you wear a garment for the first time—*before* you toss it in the washer.

Moisten the underarm area—or any other spot where perspiration stains are a problem—and work in a lather of Fels-Naptha® Laundry Bar Soap. Once you've worked up a good lather, toss the garment in the machine and launder as usual.

Working Biz® Activated Non Chlorine Bleach into the stained fabric is also effective. Just make sure to wet the offending area first!

Always treat perspiration areas on a garment *prior* to laundering. If odor is present, apply warm water to the area and work in 20 Mule Team® Borax. Let sit 30 minutes or so, then launder.

If you already have stains, try dampening the fabric with warm water and working in laundry detergent and Biz®. Let that soak about 30 minutes and launder as usual.

You can also try to clean existing stains with heated white vinegar. Spray it on the fabric and then work in 20 Mule

Team® Borax. This works well on odor as well as stains.

If the fabric has changed color, try spraying with sudsy ammonia, let sit about 15 minutes, then launder as usual.

Bear in mind that yellowed or discolored fabric may be damaged. The garment may not be salvageable.

Treat everything prior to washing for the first time and do try switching brands of antiperspirant. Never wear shirts or blouses more than one day if you have a perspiration problem. You may find that wearing natural fibers such as cottons will be less of a problem than polyester and polyester blends. If your problem is serious you may want to try underarm shields. They trap moisture before it can reach the fabric. They can be removed and thrown away each day, and can't be seen through the garment. Look for them in lingerie stores and in catalogs.

SILK SPOTS: Spots on silk are hard to remove and must be handled with care.

Dry-cleaning solvent may spot-clean silk, but you're likely to be left with a ring on the fabric. Make sure to use the blow-dryer on the spot to avoid that telltale ring.

For unusual or heavy stains, take to a professional. Too much rubbing can remove the color from silk.

STICKERS: Heat white vinegar and apply it, undiluted, directly to the fabric. Allow the vinegar to soak until the sticker can be peeled back with ease.

TOMATO-BASED STAINS (ketchup, spaghetti sauce, tomato sauce, barbecue sauce, etc.): Flush these stains well with cool water as soon as possible. Make sure you apply water to the back of the fabric. Apply white vinegar and then flush again with a forceful stream of water.

Apply Wine Away® Red Wine Stain Remover per package directions.

URINE: Fresh urine stains are fairly easy to remove. First rinse well, flushing with lots of cool water. Presoak using an enzyme powder or Biz® All Fabric Bleach. Then launder as usual.

You may also soak urine-stained fabric in salt water, then rinse and launder as usual.

If the color of the fabric has changed due to the urine, sponge the area or spray with clear ammonia, then rinse and launder as usual.

VOMIT: Shake off or scrape what you can over the toilet. Flush the fabric from the "wrong" side with cool water, using a forceful stream. Once you have removed solid matter and excess liquid, make a paste of liquid laundry soap and 20 Mule Team® Borax and vigorously scrub the fabric. Rinse with salt water, pretreat and launder as usual.

Quick treatment is important to avoid stains from foods and stomach acid.

See also the treatment mentioned for **Odors.**

WINE: Never serve red wine without having white wine; nearby! And always tend to the stain *as soon as you can!*

For red wine spills, dilute the spot with white wine; then flush with cool water and apply salt.

If no white wine is available, sprinkle heavily with salt and flush with club soda or cool water.

Applying a paste of 20 Mule Team® Borax and water usually works.

For red wine spills and other red stains, keep Wine Away® Red Wine Stain Remover on hand. It is totally non-toxic and works so fast on red wine and red stains that even I am still amazed. The directions are simple and easy. Blot up the spill, apply the Wine Away®, and watch the red stain disappear. Blot with a wet cloth. You'll thank me many times for this one!